AF530482

Public Policy and Rural Development

Hemanth Kumar Mantrawadi

ATLANTIC
PUBLISHERS & DISTRIBUTORS (P) LTD

Published by
ATLANTIC
PUBLISHERS & DISTRIBUTORS (P) LTD
7/22, Ansari Road, Darya Ganj, New Delhi-110002
Phones : +91-11-40775252, 23273880, 23275880, 23280451
Fax : +91-11-23285873
Web : www.atlanticbooks.com
E-mail : orders@atlanticbooks.com

Branch Office
5, Nallathambi Street, Wallajah Road, Chennai-600002
Phones : +91-44-64611085, 32413319
E-mail : chennai@atlanticbooks.com

Copyright © Hemanth Kumar Mantrawadi, 2012

ISBN 978-81-269-1693-1

All rights reserved. No part of this publication may be reproduced, stored in a retrieval system, transmitted or utilized in any form or by any means, electronic, mechanical, photocopying, recording or otherwise, without the prior permission of the copyright owner. Application for such permission should be addressed to the publisher.

Printed in India at Glorious Printers, A-13, D.S.I.D.C.,
Jhilmil Industrial Area, Delhi-110095

Preface

In recent years, governments of most developing counties have expressed their opinions about improving the performance of their services in view of their increasing importance and the role played by them in the strategies for national development. The rise in the expectations of the people has compelled them to adopt policies for alleviating poverty and improving the quality of life of all sections of society. The basic needs of the people are required to be met on an urgent basis. To realise these objectives, the governments of developing countries have to struggle to balance their economies, effect sustained improvement in their social systems and strengthen their political systems. They have, therefore, to ensure improvement in the relevant policies. It is taken for granted that the approaches, strategies and concepts which will contribute to this are essential. The study of public policy represents a powerful approach for this purpose.

The field of public policy has assumed considerable importance in response to the increasing complexity of technology, social organization, industrialization and urbanization. It is not only concerned with the description and explanation of the causes and consequences of government activity but also with developing scientific knowledge about the forces shaping public policy. The study of public policy and rural development helps to understand the ills prevailing in society. Public policy is an important mechanism for moving a social system from the past to the future. It helps us cope with the future.

This book attempts to study various aspects of rural development in India, including welfare programmes launched by the government for the development of the rural poor. In this work, an attempt has been made to undertake an analysis of Jawahar Rozgar Yojana programme implemented in Andhra Pradesh. It is an important component of the policy initiative towards comprehensive rural development. Besides, this study deals with the substantive examination of policy issues, including policymaking and implementation and evaluation of public policy.

The book has been written to cater to the academic requirements of students pursuing postgraduation in Political Science and those preparing for civil services examination. It will not only give them a preliminary understanding of the subject, but also enable them to develop a deeper interest in the vast growing literature on public policy.

Hemanth Kumar Mantrawadi

Acknowledgements

At the outset, I sincerely express my deep sense of gratitude to Dr. V. Krishna Rao, Reader in Political Science, S.V. Degree College, Suryapet, Nalgonda, who has been a constant source of inspiration.

I sincerely thank Prof. V. Satyanarayana, Chairman, Board of Studies, Department of Political Science, Osmania University, for his constant encouragement, help and advice. I am grateful to Prof. K. Purushotham Reddy, Head, Department of Political Science, Osmania University, for his help and guidance.

I express my thanks to Prof. F.D. Vakil, Prof. Rama S. Melkote of the Department of Political Science, Osmania University for their constant advice and help. For their valuable help and encouragement, I am grateful to Prof. P.V. Rao, I/C Director, Area Study Centre, Osmania University, and Prof. T. Tirupathi Rao of the Department of Political Science, Osmania University. My sincere, thanks are also due to the faculty and staff of the Department of Political Science, my friends and Mr. G.K. Ravi Kumar, Faculty Computer Centre for their help and assistance.

In the end, I express my deepest gratitude to my father, late Sri Kodanda Ramaiah, and mother Smt. Sushila, for their kindness and affection.

I am beholden to my children, Aryan M. Wadi, Ashitha M. Wadi and my wife Srilatha, who were a source of strength during the completion of this book.

Hemanth Kumar Mantrawadi

Contents

List of Tables

1

Introduction

The study of Public Policy has assumed considerable importance in response to the increasing complexity of the society. It is not only concerned with the consequences of government activity but also develops the knowledge about the organs shaping public policy. Public policy is an important mechanism for moving a social system from the past to the future.[1] Historically, public policy has not been the central focus of the Political Science discipline. Political scientists in the beginning were largely concerned themselves with the institutions and structure of Government and the political behaviour and process rather than the content of public policy itself.[2] However, recently the study on public policy has attained considerable prominence in political science due to scientific, professional and political purposes.[3]

The public policy analysis, as a part of political science has come to occupy an important place in recent times. Though Public Policy is a sub-area of social inquiry within the broader discipline of political science, yet it has assumed the role of a supra-discipline in modern times. It is because the functions of the government, by and large, are concerned with formulation of policies and their implementation. If any political system is marked by equilibrium between inputs and outputs, the inputs emanate from the society, while the outputs are the by-products of the governmental decision-making. Since the policy determines the future of the given society, a scientific and rational knowledge about policy making is quite relevant.

Wrong policy at a right time and right policy at a wrong time would have far-reaching effect on the political system. Therefore, it is pertinent to suggest that the policymakers are to be careful about formulating the right policies at right time, indeed, it is a very difficult task to suitably lay down sound policy measures to satisfy the aspirations of the people on the one hand, and look to the general and overall development of the society on the other. In view of the above factors, the public policy perspective has a significance place in a political system.

Public policy has come to assume vital importance in modern times. The state, through a number of policies, seeks to intervene positively in the developmental process by stimulating production and ensuring distributive justice. The entire thrust thus appears to be on improving the quality of life of all the citizens.[4] The making and execution of policy in a parliamentary democracy is also subject to a variety of pressures. Indeed, pressures are so varied and so constantly changing that often policy making is perceived to be a sort of random movement without a sense of overall direction.[5] The imperatives of parliamentary democracy demand that policy making take into account the broad acceptability of any of course action decided upon by the government. In fact, the people must accept the proposed policy if the said policy is to be effective at all. It is also observed that interest groups are quite powerful to exert pressure on the system. It is because public policies are formulated by the government that they will have a salient effect on such groups and those concerned with such policies and laws would invariably play a significant role by conceivable and inconceivable methods to make such policy favourable to their interest. The constant struggle among groups as well as masses, which indirectly influences and determines the nature of decisions taken by the political executive.

An analysis of the Indian system has reveals the importance of social, political and economic factors in crisis situations. In the internal sphere, the variables leading to proper functioning of the system have been identified as investible resources, economic growth, education, political and administrative effectiveness and development of technology. Economic, social and political policies are instruments through which the government can try and regulate the system.

Theoretical Framework

Policy-making is closely related to decision-making. However, it is not the same as decision-making. Policy-making does involve decision-making, but a decision does not necessarily constitute a policy. Decision-making often involves an identification of a problem, a careful analysis of possible alternatives and a selection of one alternative for action. Generally, decisions are taken by the administrators in their day-to-day work within the existing framework of a given policy. Policy decisions eventually taken in turn provide a sense of direction to the courses of administrative action.[6]

Policy decisions are decisions made by public officials that authorise or give direction and content to public policy actions.[7] Modern urban man is born in a state financed hospital, receives his education in a government-supported school and university, spends a good part of his time travelling on the state built transportation facilities, communicates through the post office or the quasi-public telephone systems, drinks water provided by the public taps, disposes of his garbage through the public removal system, reads library books, picnics in public parts, is protected by public police, fire and health systems, eventually, he dies, again in a hospital, and may even be buried in a public cemetery. Ideological attitudes notwithstanding, his everyday life is inextricably bound up with the government decisions on these and numerous other public services.[8] Thus, in a political system, people are affected by the number of public policies in their everyday lives. Today, public policies may deal with such substantive areas as defence, environment protection, medical care and health, education, housing, taxation, inflation, science and technology, etc. The expanding sphere of public policy is reflected in the plan documents of the Planning Commission of India. The modern state uses public policy as an important source of legitimation and justification for its existence. For, the state to-day adopts the stick and carrot approach. In fact, the present welfare state had its origin in the transformation of the state from its totally coercive character to the assumption of a developmental role.

Policy formulation does not end once a decision is reached. The implementation of a decision is as important as the policy itself. No policy formulation can assume that decisions will automatically be implemented as envisioned. Policy implementation requires a wide variety of actions such as issuing policy directives that are clear and consistent, creating organisational units and assigning personnel with the information and authority necessary to administer the policies, coordinating personnel resources and expenditures to ensure benefit to target group, and evaluating already implemented actions of the personnel. The implementation of policy, thus, involves not the end of policy making, but a continuation of policy making by other means. By and large, public policies that are formulated, are in tune with the basic objectives of the country as enshrined in the Constitution and also for bringing about a suitable transformation in society from tradition to modernity.

A comprehensive study of public policy begins with a systematic enquiry into the various forces that shape the policy which are known as the inputs into the policy. The analysis of the policy content includes the decisions and actions of the government in pursuance of the policy. The examination of the accomplishments of public policy, which is known as the policy outcome, is equally significant. It helps us to understand how far the intended results have been achieved and the whether problems appearing from time to time have been overcome.

In the final analysis, the feedback of a public policy influences the future decisions of the government. Therefore, proper analysis of public policies enables the decision-makers to choose the right policy, allocate appropriate priorities and adopt efficient measures of implementation.

We have become more aware of the policy process as a suitable object of study in its own right, primarily in the hope of improving the rationality of the flow of decisions.[9] The study of public policy has attracted greater attention of the political scientists in the contemporary times as it anlayses the causes and effects of governmental activities. The study of public policy involves an assessment of the impact of environmental forces on the content of public policy and an analysis of the effect of various institutional arrangements and political processes on public policy. It also includes an inquiry into the consequences of various public policies for the political system, and an evaluation of the impact of both expected and unexpected consequences.[10] Politically, there are the difficulties faced by the democratic, federal structure in articulating clear and unambiguous goals. This vagueness of configuration of articulation of interaction between the various political authorities ranging from the village to the central level, and the difficulties associated with future expenditure and resource use patterns being inextricably linked to past decisions. There are also the ramifications flowing from the working of a mixed economy whereby the private sector policies are responsive to government actions. The need for coordinating various policy measures such as public and private adds another dimension to policy making.

Policy Making in India

Policy making in India has to take place in the context of a complex emerging society. Any society has its own fundamentals, its own compulsions, and its own inner dynamics. The ambitious goals set for society have put it in a state of flux and change. The goals of reconstruction, including abolition of poverty, have led to increasing expectations and generated the need for rapid and orderly change. But any national advance has to be viewed within a framework of parameters flowing from (i) India being a democratic country, still an under developed Third World nation; and (ii) India being a country of vast size and population giving it a continental dimension with its various regions, linguistic groups, cultural units, minorities, etc. Rising expectations and the goals set for itself by the state, when viewed in the context of the lack of resources, underline the need for attaining optimality in both the formulation and implementation of policy.[11]

Policy making to be effective and efficient has to be preceded by policy analysis. Policy analysis, and its concomitant policy development, has many connotations. The more prevalent usage of the term includes the following:

(i) Rational and technical approach to identifying trends and predicting future scenarios as the basis of developing long range unified substantive policy alternatives for managing public affairs;

(ii) Study of decision-making dynamics in administration;

(iii) Analysis of policy planning institutions and procedures with reference to their implications for rationality and quality of policies; and

(iv) Application of scientific approach and social sciences to management of public affairs.[12]

In countries where the problem of poverty is less serious, there is great pressure on governments to accelerate national development, make use of up-to-date and relevant technological innovations, adopt and facilitate necessary institutional changes, increase national production, make full use of human and other resources, and improve the level of living.[13] These trends and developments have therefore enhanced both the size and scope of public policy.

The study of public policy has much to offer to the development of administration in different sectors of the economy. It will enable the administration to engage in such issues as are of public importance and are concerned with the transformation of values into public policy-making and demanding the meaningful actions of public servants. Social scientists, especially political scientists, manifest concern with what governments should do with appropriate public policy. They contend that political science cannot be silent on current social and political problems and that political scientists have a moral obligation to put forward a particular policy on a particular problem. They should increase the level of political knowledge and improve the qualify of public policy in whatever ways they think best, notwithstanding the fact that substantial disagreement exists in society over what constitutes appropriate policies or the right goals.[14]

Rural Development and Public Policy

Ever since the country's independence, rural development has been one of the the important policies of the government. The constant effort of the government has been to develop the rural areas where the vast majority of the people live. But the kind of development and the amount of developments, which have actually been realised, have been much below the planned aim of development. There has been no dearth of funds made available according to the allotment in different plans. The governmental policies have also been suitably modified from time to time. But the actual pace of development has been slow and much below expectation.[15]

The fundamental objective of rural development is to provide improved facilities like electrification, irrigation, communication, education, health care productivity, increased employment and higher income for the target groups, and technological changes in agriculture and allied sectors. This implies reducing poverty and human misery by increasing the productivity of the poorer sections and providing them greater access to goods and services. Further, rural development strategy needs to be explicitly identified with improving the overall quality of life of the poor masses. Rural development strategy is mainly motivated at achieving three fundamental goals:

(i) generation of self employment opportunities in rural areas through programmes which are mainly intended to provide income-generating assets to people below the poverty line;

(ii) providing employment through programmes like the National Rural Employment Programme, Rural Landless Employment Guarantee Programme, Jawahar Rozgar Yojana, etc. and improving the skills of the rural people through training and providing basic needs like drinking water, sanitation and housing, etc.;

(iii) the Government has recognised that people's involvement should be ensured at every stage of the development programmes, for a united effort in rural areas.

After the Second World War, the concept of the state in relation to its economic activities had undergone significant changes. The Union, the States and the Local Governments have increasingly participated in the economic and social functions. The state preferred to control and guide many activities.

Further, there is a shift of emphasis from revenue to welfare and from cyclical stabilisation to secular growth. The major goal of the state is social objective equalisation with regard to basic services like education, public health and medical services.[16] Since the commencement of the planning era in India in 1951, growth with social mistice has been set forth as the cardinal principle of Indian planned economic development. Indian economy is a rural economy.[17] The potentiality for progress and valuable sources lies in villages and not in a few metropolitan or municipal areas. In a predominantly agrarian economy like ours, the solution to massive problems of poverty and unemployment lies in the development of rural areas.

The objectives of rural development may broadly be defined as maximising production in agriculture and allied activities in the rural areas, development of rural industries with emphasis on village and cottage industries, generating of maximum possible employment opportunities in rural areas especially for the weaker sections in the community so as to enable them to improve their standard of living, providing basic services like drinking water, communication facilities, health and welfare, and education.

Development of rural areas has drawn attention of several Indian leaders as well as the intelligentsia in the early 1920s. A few experiments were also attempted with little success, in rebuilding all rural parts of India. Despite a few experiments, the rural areas continued to be neglected. The steady increase of population, coupled with the alien rule during pre-independent times were responsible for the neglect of rural India. Whatever progress was achieved in the past was confined to the urban parts. The benefits of progress did not reach the rural areas, particularly rural poor. After independence, attention was focused on the theme of rural development and considerable efforts were made in that direction, both by the Union and State Governments.

Several studies had convincingly shown that the powerful section of the rural population and the better endowed segments had appropriated a disproportionately large share of the benefits of development efforts. In the process, rural poverty increased instead of decreasing and the weaker sections of the society, particularly among the rural areas, continued to lead a pathetic life.[18]

It is also observed that the bureaucracy should be made to involve itself in doing certain productive works in the rural areas. The bureaucracy should start small and medium industries in rural areas, for which the private industries do not come forward. Small and medium industries in rural areas managed by the rural administration and local bodies could be a counter part of the public sector at the district level. A shift from regulatory functions to direct responsibility for production alone will help to improve the image of rural administration and rural areas as well. The control functions of bureaucracy have neither brought growth nor equity. If production-oriented economic activities at the district level and below are brought under the regulation of a control-oriented government sector, it will have a negative effect on the growth rate of our small economy.[19] Merely tinkering with the forms of administration and attitude of administrators is not going to solve the problems of rural development.

It is also observed that because of historical tradition, the Indian bureaucracy has remained regulation or control-oriented and it converts even the development functions by subtle devices. It has developed its own means of defence mechanism by allocating a large proportion of funds given for development to salaries and wages so that the elected representatives at the rural and state levels would have a small proportion of funds for allocation and economic production-oriented activities at the rural level. The rural administration should rake up small and medium industries, which the private sector does not come forward to start. This will result in the economic development of the rural areas.

Several social scientists have observed that the elite is unhelpful and that the rural elite are opposed to the development of the poor. The elite is described as selfish, corrupt and a without motivation, function ridden, partisan and exploitative in nature. This indicates the erosion of legitimacy and credibility of the rural elite. The poor have come to see through and look beyond the local elite groups.

This attitudinal pattern also knocks away the local initiative causing a leadership crisis. With the result, mass organisation and mass mobilisation become difficult until new leadership merges with greater credibility from the poor themselves.[20] Increasing governmental assistance and effective implementation of anti-poverty schemes, redistribution of land and strengthening of irrigation potential, etc. make the rural poor look to the rural government for the eradication of rural poverty.

Community Development Programme

Community Development Programme was launched in October 1952 with a view to evoking popular enthusiasm and public cooperation in the process of social and economic developments of the villages. It was conceived as basically a programme of the people, by the people and for the people with a reasonable amount of technical and financial assistance from the government. However, the Community Development Programme failed to enthuse people and enlist their participation in its functioning.

A study team under the leadership of Balwantrai Mehta was appointed in 1957 to improve the growth process on a sound footing at the rural level. The Balwantrai Mehta Committee recommended a three-tier model of Panchayat Raj to serve as an instrument of development from below. The introduction of Panchayat Raj system as an instrument of development from below, marked a turning point in planning and the implementation of the socio-economic programmes at the small level. It was introduced to provide a bold and imaginative leadership for the all-round development of the rural area. The system was conceived of and set up as an instrument of change and transformation. The three-tier representation at the rural level provided the base for the administrators, elected representatives and local population to participate in the developmental effort. The elected representative of the rural people started to play the key role in the decision-making process. The representation are regarded as facilitation of the process of rural development. Since the emphasis of rural development policies is bringing about people's participation in the development programmes, it is possible to achieve this through the elected representatives.[21] The rural administrators are expected to participate with missionary real in the life and development of the rural areas. These rural administrative institutions are to be galvanised to become effective instruments of social and economic rural development. The district level of administration has been the main instrument for the implementation of the governmental policies. This has been so since the days of the British administration and it is still the main agency through which the government works. In earlier times, the main concern of administration at this level was the maintenance of law and order and the collection of revenue. To this primary role has been added the functions of development. Consequently, the same district administration whose main concern was regulative has been made the agency of development and has to function more or less as a benefactor of the rural population. This extension in the role of the bureaucratic machinery has resulted in a dichotomy because maintenance of law and order or the collection of revenue on the one hand and the work of development implying the spending of large sums of money for improving the conditions of life in the rural area on the other hand, constitute two different roles.

The fundamental stress of the varied programmes adopted in the successive Plans has been to provide the basic and fundamental needs and necessities to the rural poor or the weaker sections of the given society. It is important to note that not only their living standards have to be improved but the environment also has to be improved. For the purpose of rural development, a plan should encompass improving productivity, increasing employment, higher income for the target groups, minimum acceptable levels of food, shelter, education and healthy atmosphere.

Dynamics of Rural Development

Rural development is viewed as the strategies, policies and programmes for the development of rural areas and promotion of activities carried out in such areas with the ultimate aim of achieving fuller utilisation of available physical and human resources and higher incomes and better living conditions for all the rural population, and particularly for the rural poor, with the effective participation of the latter in the development process.[22]

The basic task for the nation was defined as bringing about a structural transformation so as to achieve a high and sustained rate of growth, a progressive improvement in the standard of living of the rural masses loading to eradication of poverty and unemployment and to provide the material base for the overall development of the rural areas.[23] The strategy of direct attack on poverty cannot be sustained if the overall growth of the economy itself is slow and the benefits of such growth inequitably distributed. Programmes for poverty alleviation are to be regarded as supplementing the basic plan for overall economic growth in terms of generating productive assets and skills as well as incomes for the poor. Rural development, keeping the intention of the overall development of rural areas, may be defined beyond narrow economic criteria such as reduction of poverty, unemployment and inequalities, but these thrusts are to be supplemented by sustained economic growth. It may be observed that as many as 47 programmes have been introduced from 1951 till 1989.[24]

The Eighth Five-Year Plan recognized the need for integrating various anti-poverty programmes with the sectoral factors in a specified area so as to ensure sustainable increase in employment and income of the rural poor and the infrastructure and environmental development of the area.[25] In the implementation of wage employment programme, priority is to be given to activities which improve the resource-base and eco-system in the areas such as water harvesting, de-silting irrigation tanks, construction of field channels, drainage and measures for soil conservation including afforestation. Further, the Eight-Plan proposed to create minimum of 1000 million man-days each year in the form of supplementary employment under the Jawahar Rojgar Yojana.[26] It is evident that the various governments had undertaken varied measures from time to time initiating several policies to ameliorate the innumerable problems of the rural poor and also mitigate unemployment to a great extent.

Relevance of the Study

Keeping all the above issues in view, it has been proposed to study the impact of Jawahar Rozgar Yojana on the existing structure of the given society. The study has been confined to the implementation, achievements and difficulties faced in Ranga Reddy district of Andhra Pradesh.

Review of Literature

Abundant literature is available on public policy and rural development. But there appears to be a gap in research work on Jawahar Rozgar Yojna programme in Andhra Pradesh. However, the works of political and social scientists on rural development and public policy provide valuable information pertaining to this study. G. Ram Reddy and B. Haragopal's study of the Small Farmers Unemployment Agency in Andhra Pradesh is an important contribution in this area of study. This study concludes that comparatively well-to-do farmers of higher castes have been able to derive many benefits from the process of development in view of their active participation rather than the small and marginal farmers, agricultural labourers and other people belonging to the weaker sections.

This study has brought out new aspects which will be found useful in formulating beneficiary-oriented policies and programmes in future. D.K. Desai in *Management in Rural Development* has dealt with the concept of management in rural development, policies and programmes for rural development, strategy of rural development and govermental administration concerned with rural development. C. Harichandra's work on Panchayat Raj and Rural Development makes an analysis of the various functions and responsibilities that are generally delegated to Panchayat bodies by the State Governments. It has also brought out the serious mismatch between resources and functions at the local level resulting in the neglect of both maintenance and development activities. This study also highlights the fact that developmental activities such as education, water supply, and general welfare can be handled effectively by the Panchayat Raj institutions. Ch. Balaramaiah's study on Administration of Anti-Poverty programme: A Study of Small Farmers Development Agency" concluded that the bulk of the beneficiaries are not utilizing the schemes for the right purpose. On the other hand, the agencies allocation of financial assistance have not identified the proper beneficiaries. S.K. Jha's study on Rural Development Administration in India is an attempt to look at the problems from the point of view of development administration and the administration of development in rural India. The author says that the present bureaucratic model is not at all suitable to discharge its duty of a total societal transformation.

Administrative development is an integral part of social and economic development and the increasing list of bureaucracy should not itself be equated with administrative development. Administrative development occurs only if we find a bureaucracy becoming increasingly responsible for the implementation of policies formulated outside the bureaucracy. M.S. Randhawa's book *Developing Village in India* explains that with the entry of Mahatma Gandhi into the political arena, rural development received mass popular support and became inextricably linked-up with the national movement. As a result, after independence, there was a strong national consensus for stressing rural development in India. R.N. Agarwala's study on National Movement and constitutional Development of India is highly informative providing historical backdrop for the prominence given to the rural development in India. With the implementation of Montague-Chelms ford Reforms, the Provincial Governments inherited many functions of rural development under the transferred list. Consequently, the Indian Ministers gave a strong fillip to rural development in India. The Government of India Act, 1935 further institutionalised the system and conferred autonomy on the Provincial Governments.

R.K. Sapru's study on Public Policy attempts to bridge the gap between the traditional academic approaches to the study of government and thereby to relate those approaches to the outputs of government, namely public policies. This study deals with the substantive examination of policy issues, including policy-making and implementation and the evaluation of public policy. Krishan Saigal's work on Policy hating in India: An Approach to Optimisation draws upon the powerful analytical and computational techniques of the ongoing managerial revolution to develop alternative organisational patterns to articulate an integrated policy package. This study also develops a normative model of the Indian system to help understand how appropriate policies can steer society in the desired direction.

The field of public policy has assumed considerable importance in response to the increasing complexity of technology, social organsiation, socialisation and urbanisation. This is not only concerned with the description and explanation of the causes and consequences of government activity but also with developing scientific knowledge about the forces shaping public policy.

R. Scott and A. Shore's study on Why Sociology does not Apply: A Study of the Use of Sociology in Public Policy, observes that policy analysis implies such procedures which will lead to more frictionless situations than we now have, situations that maximise the good and minimise harm done to those affected by them. It is felt that policy science is ladden with utilitarianism assumptions. In *Policy Science: Analysis or Ideology*, L. Tribe argues that policy science aims at exaltation of utilization and self-interested individualism, efficiency and maximised production. Policy science involves primarily the development of professional analysts who are expert in national decision-making. It is an inter-disciplinary approach which is intended to afford these analysts objective criteria upon which policy decisions can be made.

E. Jantsch is critical of analytical approaches to policy. In his *Design for Evolution*, he argues that they are informed by an unrealistic separation between regulations and the system being regulated. According to Jantsch, the human systems can be understood merely as networks for processing information and making decisions. This approach to human systems gives rise to two related distortions:

(i) it stresses technological solutions to social problems, to the exclusion of cultural design, i.e. social change through value adoption; and

(ii) it is reductionist in that it denies that human systems are more than the sum of individual expressions of their members. Jantsch contends that society and its sub-systems possess a life far richer and deeper, a life which heightens, magnifies, focuses, and restrains the life of all the human members which express themselves through these systems. Hence, Jantsch suggests an alternative approach to policy-making, involving social regulation through deliberate adoption of the appreciative system.

A few research articles on the Jawahar Rozgar Yojana Programmes have appeared in leading journals and periodicals. Some of those are worth mentioning in this context. Hari Prakash Maheshwari's article entitled "Jawahar Rozgar Yojana: A Case Study in Bulandshar District, U.P", in which he observed that workers were not available at wage rates prescribed by the government and majority of the villages are aware of the scheme but ignorant about its details. Ranjit Sen's study on "Rural Poverty: A Tentative Hypothesis" concludes that minimum wages have no menial unless at the same time somebody guarantees employment at the described minimum wage. Raj Krishna's study entitled "Review of SFDA: Philosophy and Performance" pointed out that landless labourers and farmers with less than five acres of dry land constituted the hard core of rural poverty and population.

Garry D. Brewer's *Politicians, Bureaucrats, and the Consultant—A Critique of Urban Problem Solving*, Thomas R. Dye's *Understanding Public Policy*, R.R. Burt's *Policy Analysis: Introduction and Applications to Health Programme Public Sector*, L.L. Wade and R.L. Curry's *A Logic of Public Policy: Aspects of Political Economy*, Randall B. Riplay's *Congress: Process and Policy*, S.R. Maheshwari's *Public Policy Making in India*, K. Santhanam's *Union State Relation in India*, Charles E. Lindblom's *The Policy-making Process*, Rajeshwar Dayal's *Community Development Programme in India*, Pareek Udai's *Some Aspects of Social Change in India*, Narendeshwar Prasad's *Change Strategy in a Developing Society: India*, K.N. Prasad's *The Economics of a Backward Region in a Backward Economy* and R.C. Prasad's *Democracy and Development: The Grassroot Experience in India* are some of the needful material providing much information about public policy and rural development. The gap that exists today insofar as research work on Jawahar Rozgar Yojana Programme will to some extent be fulled up though the present work.

Objectives

Rural development in India involves various programmes for the development of the rural poor. It was realised that poverty and Unemployment had increased and there was an increasing agrarian tension threatening to turn the Green Revolution into a Red Revolution. There are some political commitments to eradication of poverty as voiced in the slogan Garibi Hatao of Smt. Indira Gandhi's policies during the mid-term elections to Lok Sabha in 1971. It was felt that unless specially designed programmes for selected target groups are implemented, there is little chance of the poorer beneficiaries sharing the benefits of the development. In this work, an attempt is made to undertake an analysis of Jawahar Rozgar Yojana Programme implemented in the Ranga Reddy district in Andhra Pradesh. The Jawahar Rojgar Yojana is an important component of the policy initiative towards comprehensive rural development. The existing wage employment programmes were merged into the new programmes named as Jawahar Rojgar Yojana intensive wage employment programme in backward districts with acute poverty and unemployment. The primary objective of Jawahar Rojgar Yojana is generation of additional gainful employment for the unemployed and underemployed individuals in the rural areas. The main objectives of the study are:

(i) to examine the impact and performance of Jawahar Rozgar Yojana Programme in Ranga Reddy district;

(ii) to identify the beneficiaries in Ranga Reddy district;

(iii) to examine the socio-economic political background of the beneficiaries in Ranga Reddy district;

(iv) to focus on the targets, achievements and difficulties experienced at field level implementation;

(v) to study the impact of the programme on village level politics, and

(vi) to get suggestions from the beneficiaries in Ranga Reddy district to make the Jawahar Rozgar Yojana more effective at the rural level.

Methodology

In the following paragraphs the researcher makes an attempt to bring out the methodology used in the study. The methodology adopted for this work is a combination of both empirical and historical techniques. The study also employed multi-staged purposive random sampling technique. Since the study proposes to examine the impact of the programme on the beneficiaries, it was attempted to cover certain beneficiaries giving representation to all walks of life of the individuals in the society. This was thought as necessary to gain insight into the problems faced in targeting the scheme and its implementation. In the absence of coverage of a large number of beneficiaries, it is observed that the study would not be able to generate adequate information on the aspects that the study seeks to cover. Hence, it is proposed to interview 300 beneficiaries those connected with the formulation, implementation of the programme at the grassroot level and also those belonging to the target group.

The researcher also makes an attempt to examine the impact of different schemes under this programme and also their viability. This is considered important to analyse the suitability and effectiveness of a public policy for removal of poverty. Participation of the target groups in the implementation of the policies is examined. This is considered vital for the success of a public policy like the Jawahar Rozgar Yojana Programme. For this purpose the attitudinal pattern of the beneficiaries is examined on the basis of which the emerging pattern is discerned.

In this study, the researcher makes an effort to examine the working of the Jawahar Rozgar Yojana in a larger perspective and wider socio-economic context. It is hoped that this would provide an insight into the working of the schemes necessary to improve the existing understanding of public policy for target group development. In all 300 respondents were interviewed with the help of a questionnaire specially designed for the purpose of collecting the information. The questionnaire was referred to a few experts and persons having field experience. In addition to the interview schedules informal discussions were also held with those officials and political elites who had fruitful information which would be of use for this study. In addition to this, the researcher also adopted the non-participant observation technique in order to study the working of the programme from close quarters. The factual and relevant data was collected from secondary sources. The study examines the phenomenon basically from a public policy angle and attempts to explain the gap between the policies and performance.

Chapterisation

The study on Public Policy and Rural Development—A Study of Jawahar Rozgar Yojana in Ranga Reddy District is spread over six chapters. This chapter contains the theoretical background about public policy, rural development, review of literature, objectives of the study and the methodology adopted for this study.

The Second Chapter is devoted for the discussion on the profile of the Ranga Reddy district in Andhra Pradesh.

The Third Chapter focuses attention on the components of Jawahar Rozgar Yojana Programme.

An attempt is made in the Fourth Chapter to make evaluation of the implementation and performance of Jawahar Rozgar Yojana in Ranga Reddy district.

The last chapter brings together and presents briefly the salient features and findings of the study. Some relevant suggestions are also made to make Jawahar Rozgar Yojana Programme effective in promoting rural development and welfare.

Notes

1. R.K. Sapru, *Public Policy*, Sterling Publishers, New Delhi, 1994, p. 14.
2. Thomas R. Dye, *Policy Analysis*, University of Alabama Press, Alabama, 1976, p. 2.
3. Thomas R. Dye, *Understanding of Public Policy*, Princeton Hail Inc., Englewood Cliff, New Jersey, 1972, p. 2.
4. Ram Reddy G. and Haragopal G., *Public Policy and the Rural Poor in India*, Concept Publishing Company, New Delhi, 1985, p. 1.
5. Kishan Saigal, *Policy Making in India*, Vikas Publishing House Pvt. Ltd., New Delhi, 1983, p. 4.
6. R.K. Sapru, *Public Policy*, *op. cit.*, p. 14.
7. James E. Anderson, *Public Policy-Making*, Praeger, New York, 1975, p. 4.
8. Michael Teitz, "Towards a Theory of Urban Public Facility Location", Papers of the Regional Science Association, No. 21, 1968, p. 36.
9. Harold D. Lasswell, "Public Policy Orientation", in Leaner, D. and Lasswell, H.D. (eds.), *The Policy Science*, Stanford, California, p. 3.
10. Thomas R. Dye, *op. cit.*, p. 5.

11. Kishan Saigal, *op. cit.*, p. 5.
12. A.M. Banerjee and Faquir Mohammad, "Policy Analysis and Development, in S.K. Sharma, *Dynamics of Development*, Concept Publishing Co., Delhi, 1977, pp. 467-68.
13. *Development Administration: Current Approaches and Trends in Public Administration for National Development*, Department of Economics and Social Affairs, United Nations, New York, 1975, p. 9.
14. R.K. Sapru, *Public Policy*, *op. cit.*, p. 14.
15. S.K. Jha, *Rural Development Administration in India*, Janaki Prakashan, New Delhi, 1988, p. 1.
16. C. Harichandran, *Panchayat Raj and Rural Development*, Concept Publishing Co., New Delhi, 1983, p. 25.
17. Government of India, *India—A Reference Annual 1976*, New Delhi, 1976, p. 12.
18. For details see: Vasant Desai, *Rural Development: Programmes and Strategies*, Himalaya Publishing House, Bombay, 1988.
19. D.K. Desai, *Management in Rural Development*, Oxford & IBH Publishing Co., New Delhi, 1983, pp. 131-33.
20. Ram Reddy G. and Haragopal G., *Public Policy and the Rural Poor*, *op. cit.*, p. 237.
21. B.C. Muthayya, K. Krishanama Naidu, and M. Aneeruddin, *Behavioural Dimensions of Rural Leaders*, National Institute of Rural Development, Hyderabad, 1979, p. 1.
22. P. George, "Employment Generation: Early Experiments", Paper Presented to National Workshop on JRY, NIRD, July 1990.
23. For discussion on rural development see:
    (a) D.I. Narayana, "The Rural Development Programme and Poverty Eradication", Paper Presented at Seminar on NREP and RLEGP, Ministry of Rural Development, Government of India, New Delhi, Feb. 27-28, 1989.
    (b) N. Kakwani and K. Subba Rao, "Rural Poverty and Its Alleviation in India", *Economic, and Political Weekly*, Vol. XXV, No. 13, March 31, 1990, pp. A-2-16.
    (c) C.H. Hanumanth Rao, "Integrating Poverty Alleviation Programme with Development Strategies: Indian Experience", *Economic and Political Weekly*, Vol. XXVII, No. 48, November 28, 1992, pp. 2603-07.

25. Planning Commission, *Eighth Five Year Plan*, Vol. II, Government of India, New Delhi, p. 37.
26. Vasant Desai, *Rural Development: Programme and Strategies*, *op. cit.*, p. 60.

2

A Profile of Ranga Reddy District

History

Ranga Reddy district comprises erstwhile Hyderabad (rural) district and was formed on 15 August 1978, by carving out some portion of Hyderabad urban taluk and the merger of the rural and urban areas of the remaining taluks of Hyderabad district. Therefore, the history of Ranga Reddy is none other than the history of Hyderabad.

The Nizam State

Kakatiyas of Warangal were the first important rulers of this part of the country between 1150-1323. Muhammad-bin-Tughlak who broke the Kakatiya power in 1323, held sway for some time, after which the royal court of the Bahmani sultans held the Deccan for about two centuries. On their decline, the Barid Shahi Kingdom rose to power which, for unknown reasons, dwindled by about 1609. Then came the famous Qutub Shahis of Golconda (1512-1687) whose rule opened a glorious chapter in the annals of Hyderabad. It was in the reign of the fifth descendant of this dynasty, Mohammed Quli, that the nucleus of the Hyderabad city, renowned for its magnificent mansions, had been laid in 1589. However, towards the close of the 17th century the fortress of Golconda fell to the sword of Aurangazeb (1687) who made it a part and parcel of the Mughal Empire and nominated Chin Kalich Khan (Asaf Jah) as Subedar of the Deccan, who in turn, made himself the master of the Deccan after defeating Mubariz

Khan, in the famous battle of Shakarkheda fought on the 11 October 1724. This battle which was renamed as Fathkhera by the Nizam-ul-Mulk marks the establishment of an autonomous Deccan. This famous battle saw the end of the Mughal hegemony in Deccan and the establishment of the Asaf Jah rule.

The state and the dynasty so founded by Asaf Jah I witnessed many eventful things in the evolution of the Hyderabad state. He also instituted the title of the Nizam which had become since then the hereditary and dynastic title of the successive rulers of this State and thus, he became the founder of the house of the Nizams (1724). Thereafter, the district remained as a part of the Nizam's Dominions until the merger of the Nizam State into the Indian Union in 1948. It was finally merged in the enlarged State of Andhra Pradesh on the 1 November 1956.

Early Hindu Period

In pre-historic times, the great Dravidian race occupied Southern India including a major portion of the Deccan plateau. During the Aryan era, Deccan became part of the King of Mauryan Emperor Asoka (273-31 BC). The Andhras were the next kings who ruled the Deccan. They are mentioned in the Mauryan inscriptions. Gradually, extending their sway from Krishna delta, they soon possessed an empire reaching to Nasik. This dynasty's rule came to an end in the third century.

The next dynasty of importance is that of the Chalukyas who rose to power in Bijapur district by about 550 AD and founded an empire spreading east and west across the peninsula with their capital at Kalyani. Pulakasin II (608-42 AD) ruled practically the whole of the region south of Narmada river and even came into contact with Harsha Vardhana of Kanuj. Throughout their period of supremacy, the Chalukyas were at war with the Pallavas. In the middle of eighth century, the Chalukyas were displaced by Rashtrakutas of Malhed in Gulburga district. About 973 AD, the Chalukya dynasty was restored and for nearly two hundred years maintained its position in spite of fierce struggles with Cholas and Hoyasalas of Dorasamudra. The Chalukya power fell about 1189 AD to Hoyasalas and Yadavas, the latter of whom established themselves at Deogiri. Yadavas were the last Hindu rulers of Deccan for the Vijayanagar Kingdom which was founded half a century later after the advent of the Muhammadans, never acquired much sway in the Deccan proper.

Muhammadan Period

Ala-ud-din Khilji led the first Muhammadan expedition into the Deccan in 1294 against the Yadava ruler of Deogiri and coerced him into submission. In 1296, he assassinated his own uncle and seized the throne, and sent an other expedition to Deogiri. His first expedition was dispatched in 1303 against the Kakatiya kings of Warangal, who had established themselves there since the middle of the 12th century. This having failed he sent a second expedition under Malik Kafur in 1309, which resulted in the submission of the Raja who agreed to pay tribute. Muhammad-bin-Tughlak conducted a later campaign against Warangal and finally broke the Kakatiya power in 1323. In 1310, Malik Kafur was sent against the Hyasala Raja of Dorasamudra (Helebid in Mysore). In 1318, when Harpal, the Deogiri ruler rebelled, he was defeated and put to death and with him the Yadava dynasty ended.

When Muhammad-bin-Tughlak ascended the throne in 1325 at Delhi, Muhammadans were masters of the Deccan from North to South. The Chief Rajas of Telangana acknowledged their sway and paid tribute. Tughlak changed the name of Deogiri to Daulatabad and made it his capital. A few years later, the Imperial Governors of the Deccan revolted resulting in the establishment of the Bahmani dynasty. Zafar Khan, who styled himself as Ala-ud-din Hasan Shah Gangu founded this line and having taken possession of the Deccan provinces including Bidar and Gulbarga, he made Gulbarga his capital and commenced to reign from 1347 AD. The Bahmani Kingdom extended from Berar in the north to the left bank of the Tungabhadra in the south and from Dabal on the west coast to Telangana tracts in the east.

After the fall of this dynasty, the Barid Shahi dynasty came into power. Amir Barid who assumed sole charge of the affairs of the Bahmani Kingdom after the downfall of the Bahmani dynasty had many vicissitudes and constant wars with the rulers of Bijapur and Berar and he died in Daulatabad in 1538. He was succeeded by his son Ali Barid who was the first to assume the title of Shah. In 1565, he marched along with the other Deccan kings against the Rajas of Vijayanagar and in the memorable battle of Tallikota the Vijayanagar ruler was defeated and his fate was sealed. Ali Barid died in 1582 and he was succeeded by three other kings.

The Qutub Shahi dynasty next came into prominence. Qutub-ul-Mulk Sultan Kuli, a Turk of noble family who was Governor of the Golconda province under the Bahmanis, took advantage of the distracted state of the kingdom under Muhammad Shah of the Barid Shahi dynasty and declared his independence through establishing the Qutub Shahi dynasty which reigned from 1512 to 1687 AD.

When the Mughals invaded the Deccan, the local rulers formed an alliance against them, but after defeating the invaders they fell out among themselves, enabling the Mughal troops to subject the country. Shah Jahan, after rebelling against his father fled from Buthanpur and was welcomed at Golconda by Abdullah Qutub Shah. In 1635 AD, Shah Jahan who had then become the emperor, sent a farmana to Golconds which was well received. Mir Jumla, the King's minister, appealed to Aurangzeb for help against his master in 1655 A.D. and this afforded a pretext for Aurangzeb to invade the territory, Hyderabad was plundered, but Abdullah settled for peace and paid arrears of tribute. He died in 1674 AD. He was succeeded by his nephew Afjal Hasan, who was also called Tana Shah. After the fall of Bijapur in 1686 AD, Aurangzeb turned his attention to Golconda which was taken in the following year. Tana Shah was made a prisoner and died in 1704 AD and with him the Qutub Shahi line ended. This dynasty was followed by Asaf Jahi dynasty to which the later Nizams belonged.

The Asaf Jahi dynasty was founded by Asaf Jah, a distinguished General of Aurangzeb, a Turkman by descent. After a long service under the Delhi emperor, he was appointed as Subedar or Viceroy of the Deccan in 1713 AD with the title of Nizam-ul-Mulk which has since become the hereditary title of the family.

The Mughal empire at this period was on the verge of decline owing to internal dissensions and attacks from without. Amidst the general confusion, Asaf Jah had little difficulty in asserting his independence against the weak Mughals of Delhi, but he had to content with Marathas who were harassing the west of his newly acquired territories. The Governor of Khandesh Mubariz Khan opposed Asaf Jah. A battle was fought at Shakark holds in the Buldana district of Berar in 1724 AD in which Mubariz Khan was totally defeated and lost his life. This battle established the independence of Asaf Jah who annexed Berar and fixed his residence at Hyderabad and established his dominions. The Hyderabad district along with the rest of the Telangana came under the control of the Asaf Jahi dynasty.

After the death of Asaf Jah, Nazir Jung, his second son and Muzaffar Jung, his grandson, strove for the succession. At this time the English and the French were contending for supremacy in the East and each of the claimants secured the support of one of these powers; Nazir Jung's cause was espoused by the English, while Muzaffar Jung was supported by the French. The latter, however, was imprisoned by his uncle, but on the assassination of Nazir Jung, Muzaffar Jung was proclaimed the sovereign. Dupleix, the French Governor, became the controller of the Nizam's authority. Muzaffar Jung was killed by some Pathan Chiefs and the French then selected Salabat Jung a brother of Nazir Jung and son of Asaf Jah as ruler. Ghazi-ud-Din, the eldest son of Asaf Jah, who, it was alleged had relinquished his claim at first but now appeared as a claimant, supported by the Marathas, but his sudden death put an end to further struggles. The English and the French were then contesting for power and influence in the Deccan, but the victories of Clive in the Carnatic caused the latter to turn their attention to their own possessions. Nizam Ali Khan, the fourth son of Asaf Jah, at this juncture obtained the support of the English on the promise of dismissing the French presence from his service. Salabat Jung was dethroned in 1761 AD and Nizam Ali Khan was proclaimed ruler.

In 1766 AD, the Northern Circars were ceded to the British on the condition that the Nizam was to be furnished with a subsidiary force in time of war and received six lakhs of rupees per annum when no troops were required. The Nizam on his part promising to support the British with his troops. This was followed by the treaty of 1768 AD, by which the East India Company and the Nawab of Carnatic engaged to assist the Nizarn with troops whenever required by him on payment. In 1790 AD, war broke out between Tipu Sultan and the British and a treaty of alliance was concluded between the Nizam, the Marathas and the British. Tipu, however, concluded peace and had to relinquish hold of his dominions which were divided among the allies. In 1798 AD, another treaty was concluded between the Nizam and the British. After the fall of Seringapatnam and the death of Tipu Sultan, the Nizam participated largely under the treaty of Mysore in 1799. In the division of territory and his share was increased because of the withdrawal of the Peshwar from the treaty. In 1800, a fresh treaty was concluded between the Nizam and the British by which Nizam ceded all the territories which had accrued to him under the treaties of 1792, and 1799, i.e. Cuddapah, Kurnool, Anantapur and Bellary districts, known as the Ceded Districts of Madras.

Nizam Ali Khan died in 1803 and he was succeeded by his son, Sikandar Jah. After the death of Sikandar Jah in 1829, his son Nasir-ud-Doula succeeded. Nasir-ud-Doula died in May 1857 and he was succeeded by his son Afzal-ud-Doula. In 1869, after the death of Afzal-ud-Doula, his son Mir Mahbub Ali Khan Bahadur became the ruler. As he was only three years old then, a regency was constituted for the administration of the country, with Salar Jung I as Regent and Nawab Sham-ul-Umara as Co-Regent. The British Resident was consulted on all important matters concerning the welfare of the State. On the death of the Co-Regent in 1877, his elder brother Nawab Vikar-ul-Umara was appointed as co-administrator but he also died in 1881. Sir Salar Jung remained as the sole administrator and Regent till his death in 1883. In 1884, Mir Mahabub Ali Khan was installed as ruler by Lord Rippon. After the death of Mir Mahbub Ali Khan, in 1911, Mir Osman Ali Khan ascended the throne. In 1947, when India attained independence, Princely states were given the choice either to remain independent or to join the Indian Union. The Nizam's Dominions became part of Indian Union in 1948 consequent to Police Action. In 1956, during the re-organisation of States, the Hyderabad State was bifurcated and the nine predominantly Telugu speaking districts of Mahabubnagar, Hyderabad, Medak, Nizamabad, Adilabad, Karimnagar, Warangal, Khamman and Nalgonda known as the Telangana region were transferred to Andhra Pradesh.

Geography

Ranga Reddy district is mostly hilly and sparsely wooded. The general slope of the land is from west to east and southeast. The Rajkonda hill range runs in a south-eastern direction upto Devarakonda Mandal in Nalgonda district. The Anantagiri range traverses the district from the south in Mahabubnagar district to the north upto Dharur. A large portion of this range is composed of high grade laterite. Isolated granite hills are also found here and there. The climate of Ranga Reddy district is relatively moderate. It is generally hot and dry. Consequently, the flora of the district exhibits xerophytic adaptations. About 42.5 per cent of the land in the district is under cultivation. The uncultivated patches, the hills and slopes are generally covered by some sort of growth.

Ranga Reddy district cannot boast of any important timber yielding forests because of the low rainfall and comparatively inferior soil conditions, aggravated by the ever increasing biotic interference. The soils have very little plant nutrients and so they support only very inferior type of forests. The forest area, in this district covers about 9.7 per cent of the total geographical area of the district, as against the minimum of 33.5 per cent desirable according to the National Forest Policy. The forests are of crop type, where the trees are generally of stunted growth and malformed. Naturally, regeneration is practically absent on account of the unchecked grazing by herds of cattle, goats and sheep, and frequent occurrence of fires. The forests of the district are broadly classified into forest types based on the All-India classification as southern tropical Dry Deciduous Forests.

Rivers, Canals and Waterways

The chief river of the district is Musi, which rises in the Anantagiri hills near Sivareddipet village (Vicarabad Revenue Mandal). It flows almost due east passing through the middle of Hyderabad city, into Nalgonda district where it joins the Krishna river near Vadapalle. A reservoir called the Osmansagar across the Musi and another called the Himayathsagar across the Musi, situated at a distance of 19.31 km and 9.66 km respectively, supply of drinking water to Hyderabad city. Another river called Kagna rises in the former Vicarabad taluk (Mandal) and it drains a number of villages in the erstwhile Vicarabad and Tandur taluks.

Climate

The summer season starts in the district by about middle of March and continues till the first week of June. The heat in April and May is very severe. The south west monsoon season is very severe which begins in the first week of June and extends up to the end of September. December to February is winter season in this district. The average annual rainfall in the district is 802.1 mm.

Temperature

The records at the meteorological observatory in the district at Begumpet may be taken as a representative of the meteorological conditions prevailing in the district in general. From about mid-February both the day and night temperatures begin to increase steadily. May is the hottest month with the mean daily maximum temperature at 39.6°C (103.3°F). From June onwards, there is appreciable drop in temperatures with the onset of the south-west monsoon and the weather becomes more pleasant. By the beginning of November, the decrease in both the day and night temperatures is rapid. December is the coldest month with the mean daily maximum temperature at 28.6°C (83.8°F) and the mean daily minimum temperature at

13.6°C (56.5°F). In this season, the night temperature drops down to about 7°C (44.6°F). The highest maximum temperature recorded at Begumpet was 44.4°C (111.9°F) on the 28 May 1985. The lowest minimum was 6.1°C (43.0°F) on the 8 January 1946.

During the south-west Monsoon season, the relative humidities are generally high, ranging between 70 to 80 per cent on the average. Humidity decreases from post monsoon season onwards. The driest part of the year is the summer season when the humidity is generally between 30 to 35 per cent in the afternoon.

During the south-west monsoon season, the skies are generally heavily clouded or overcast; the cloudiness decreases in the post-monsoon season. The skies are mostly clear or lightly clouded in the succeeding seasons.

Red Soils

Red soils predominate in the district followed by black soils. The mandals where more than 50 per cent of the villages have red chalk soils as the predominant soils are in Medchal, Shamirpet, Qutubullapura Kessara, Hayatnagar, Saroornagar, Uppal and Ghatkesar, Rajendranagar, Pargi, Doma Sharmhabad; Sherlingampally, Malkajgiri, Balanagar, Kulkacherla and Ganded. Dubba soils are largely found in Ibrahimpatnam, Manchal, Yacharam, Maheshwaram and Kandukur mandals besides red chalk soils. The mandals where the soils are predominantly black are Chevella, Shahbad, Shankarpally, Moinabad, Vikarabad, Nawabpet, Dharror, Pudur, Tandur, Peddamul, Yalal Bashirabad, Marpally, Mominpet and Bantaram.

Minerals

In Ranga Reddy district, quartz and felspar are the principal minerals of economic importance. Good quality of quartz used for the glass industry is found within easy reach of Hyderabad city. The extensively exploited quartz are available in the mandals of Medchal, Maheshwaram, Rajendranagar, Malkagiri and Pargi. The felspar is the second important mineral available in the mandals of Medchal, Hayatnagar,

Maheshwaram and Rajenderanagar around the district headquarters.

Fauna

It is on record that in 1900 the district with its low shrubbery jungles was the home of leopards, bears hyenas, occasionally tigers, while in the more open plains the antelopes were in plenty. The game reserves for the rulling family in the erstwhile Hyderabad State were stocked with these animals for the exclusive enjoyment of the nobles.

Now the forest area has receded into narrow pockets and so also the game reserves. Blackbuck, Chital or spotted deer and Sambar can still be seen in the Rasanam in Dharur, Gingurthi, Tattepalli, Nagulapally, Tirumalapur, Naskal forest blocks because of their interior location far away from Hyderabad city. Wild boar is found all over the forests. Jackal and fox are common even now in the Dharur forest area. Peacock, our National Bird and Jungle fowl are seen in the Ananthagiri Hills. Patridges and wild pigeons are common. In the cold season, wild duck, geese, teal and snipe can be seen in the small and large tanks of the district.

Thus, the geographical features contribute to the study of geopolitics of the district, geography, topography, location, forest area, mineral resources, climatic conditions, monsoon and other important factors have been discussed in detail because these factors would reflect on the political process of the district.

Table 2.1: Revenue Mandals and Municipalities

Sl. No.	Name of the Division	No. of revenue Mandals	No. of Municipalities
1.	Hyderabad East	13	4
2.	Chevella Division	13	5
3.	Vikarabad Division	11	2

Source: Ranga Reddy District Hand Book, 1995

Revenue Divisions

Ranga Reddy district is divided into 37 revenue mandals with 1055 villages and 583 Gram Panchayats. There are three revenue divisions, viz. Hyderabad East, Chevella and

Vikarabad. There are 37 mandals, which comprise 982 habitated villages and 73 unhabitated villages.

Population

Ranga Reddy district is the smallest in geographical area but the third most populous district in Andhra Pradesh. In 1971, the population of the district was 1,19,223 lakhs with increased to 15,82,062 lakhs by 1981. Further, it rose to 25,51,966 lakhs in 1991. There has been tremendous growth of population since 1991. Table 2.2 shows the growth of the population of Andhra Pradesh and Ranga Reddy since 1971.

Table 2.2: Growth Rate of Population

Sl. No.	Year	Andhra Pradesh	Ranga Reddy District
1.	1971	43502708	1109225
2.	1981	53549673	1582062
3.	1991	66508008	2551966

Source: Census Report, 1991

The sex ratio during the period 1971 to 1991 is presented in Table 2.3.

Table 2.3: Sex Ratio: Female per 1000 Males

Sl. No.	Year	Andhra Pradesh	Ranga Reddy District
1.	1971	977	967
2.	1981	975	955
3.	1991	972	941

Source: *A.P. Year Book*, 1993, Data News, Hyderabad

It is evident that males maintained their numerical superiority over females except in 1971.

Table 2.4: Population of Different Categories

Sl. No.	Category of Population	Population
1.	Male	13,06,589
2.	Female	12,30,538
3.	Scheduled Caste	3,80,000
4.	Scheduled Tribe	73,000

Source: Census of India, 1991

Ranga Reddy district is the smallest in geographical area but the third most populous district of Andhra Pradesh. The population of the district as per the 1991 Census is 25,37,127 as against 15.82 lakhs in 1981. The population has increased by nearly 9.56 lakhs during the decade. The density of population is 337 per sq. km. The details of population of the district is furnished in Table 2.4.

In the total population, 43.40 per cent belong to the labour class in which 28.70 per cent are agriculture labourers and the remaining 37.80 per cent are in different professions.

Table 2.5 reveals the rural and urban population of the district for the last three decades.

Table 2.5: Rural and Urban Population

Sl. No.		Andhra Pradesh	Ranga Reddy District
1.	1971: Rural	33.50	34.86
	1971: Urban	84.03	26.86
2.	1981: Rural	410.62	45.20
	1981: Urban	124.87	40.36
3.	1991: Rural	486.20	52.78
	1991: Urban	17.88	47.22

Source: Census of India, 1991

Table 2.6 reveals variations in the growth of population and mandal-wise analysis of population.

Table 2.6: Area and Population—Variation Population

Year	Population	Variation	Density of Population per sq.km.
1971	11,09,225	—	148
1981	15,82,062	+4,72,837	211
1991	25,28,000	+9,46,000	377

Source: Census of India, 1991

Table 2.7 gives details about the mandal-wise analysis of population.

The principal religious groups in the district are Hindus, Muslims and Christians. Hindus are in overwhelming majority in the district. The population of the Muslim community is proportionately higher in the urban and town areas of Tandur, Vikarabad, Medchal, Ibrahimpatnam, Pargi, Dharur, Shabad and Bushirbad. The population of Christians is also fairly significant in the district. Christianity in the rural areas of the

Table 2.7: Mandal-wise Analysis of Population in Ranga Reddy District: 1981-1991

Sl.No.	Name of Mandal	No. of Gram Panchayats	Revenue Villages	Population 1981	Population 1991	Male 1991	Female 1991
1.	Tandur	19	36	27055	37841	19014	18825
2.	Vikarabad	17	26	20832	25861	13131	12730
3.	Marpally	18	29	32400	41231	21159	20072
4.	Mominpet	20	26	31184	36960	18779	18181
5.	Dharur	22	38	22620	35774	18045	17729
6.	Peddemul	18	34	33690	41667	20870	20797
7.	Bashirabad	15	32	28132	34888	17287	17601
8.	Yalal	19	36	27616	33879	16748	17131
9.	Bantwaram	17	20	24087	29574	14915	14659
10.	Nawabpet	16	22	29686	37900	19244	18656
11.	Pudur	17	34	29932	73828	38717	35111
12.	Saroornagar	12	18	59198	73828	38717	35111
13.	Qutballapur	9	13	18959	28169	14860	13306
14.	Medchal	18	29	36000	46647	23975	22672
15.	Maheswaram	17	33	37011	46863	23075	22838
16.	Manchal	14	25	31423	37116	19071	18035
17.	Kesara	10	16	21048	27217	14066	13151
18.	Ibrahimpatnam	17	35	46027	57896	27800	28096
19.	Kandukur	16	30	35178	44413	22903	21510
20.	Yacharam	17	24	36313	42911	22069	20842
21.	Shamirpet	20	30	46375	55534	28515	26819
22.	Ghatkeser	12	22	35869	44978	23434	21544
23.	Hayatnagar	23	41	53869	59605	31317	28188
24.	Chevella	28	36	38925	49946	25576	24430
25.	Pargi	20	37	38565	46172	19244	18656
26.	Rajendernagar	13	19	24121	31933	16664	15269
27.	Doma	13	28	28896	35413	17684	17729
28.	Gandeed	22	29	39158	48771	24324	24447
29.	Shamshabad	22	43	44970	59629	30821	28808
30.	Shankerpally	20	26	39046	50082	25791	24291
31.	Kulkacherla	22	30	37580	46550	23369	23181
32.	Moinabad	19	26	36034	45811	23666	22145
33.	Shabad	21	25	37296	43360	22059	21301

Source: Zilla Parishad Office, Ranga Reddy district

district was introduced in 1911 in Vikarabad, Moinabad and Tandur areas. The American Missionaries started propagating Christianity in the rural areas by establishing community health services and English medium schools which have been gradually reduced after independence and the re-organisation of the linguistic states. There is a wide spread growth of the Hindu population in the Ranga Reddy district, particularly in the rural areas. The Christian population is gradually increasing in the rural areas of the district due to the fact that several English medium educational institutions are being introduced by the Christian community which paved the way for the growth of Christianity in Ranga Reddy district.

A comparative picture of the Scheduled Caste population of the district with that of the state average is presented in Table 2.8.

Table 2.8: Scheduled Caste Population

Sl. No.		Andhra Pradesh	Ranga Reddy District
1.	1971: Total	535.50	158.21
	1981: Total	663.53	255.20
2.	1981: SCs	77.62	3.08
	1991:	112.00	4.39
3.	1981: Growth of (%)	23.82	42.63
	1991: Growth of (%)	37.88	61.30
4.	1981: Growth of SCs (%)	14.87	35.36
	1991: Growth of SCs (%)	16.89	42.68

Source: *Hand Book of Statistics of Ranga Reddy District*, 1983-84 and 1990-91

It is evident that presently the Schedule Caste population of the district is 42.68 per cent, which is much more when compared to the state average of 16.89 per cent.

Scheduled Castes

The Scheduled Caste population (3,70,780) is very high in the economically backward Ranga Reddy district. They constitute a higher ratio in Malkajgiri (34.1 per cent), Bantaram (30.3 per cent), Nawabpet (27.1 per cent), Marpally (26.5 per cent) followed by Yacharam, Kandukur, Chevella, Moinabad, Pudur and Mominpet mandals. The rest of the mandals constitute less than 20 per cent of the local population. Balanagar accounts for the lowest percentage of 4.8 per cent of the Scheduled Caste population in the district.

The Scheduled Castes are mainly Malas and Madigas. These two live as separate groups in the villages. Though Malas and Madigas constitute two separate groups socially, both of them are economically downtrodden. Their separation is so distinct that Malas will not eat and drink water in Madiga's houses. There is a Kulapedda (head of the caste) in each caste who is considered as their official head and solves all the disputes and performs marriages within the community.

The Scheduled Castes in the rural areas work as agriculture labourers, or take up the traditional trades like shoe-making and tanning and other professional works. It is observed that the literacy rate among the Malas in increasing, as a result of which they could dominate over the Madigas in different fields. Due to modernization and cultural renaissance, Malas could project better leadership qualities and most of them are entering into power politics. A majority of Malas are able to enjoy better employment opportunities in state services. At least ten per cent of the Mala community appear in the Service Commission competitive examinations. But in case of Madigas, the trend is not so encouraging due to lack of education and socio-economic factors.

The Schedule Tribe population of the district compared to the state average is presented in Table 2.9.

It may be pointed out that the total Schedule Tribe population of the district accounts for 5.56 per cent which is slightly less than the state average of 9.5 per cent.

Scheduled Tribal Population

The Scheduled Tribal population (1,10,640) is very high in Kulkacherla Mandal of the district, covering 17.8 per cent followed by Manchal Mandal (16.4 per cent), Bashirabad (15.4 per cent) and Gandeed (12.1 per cent). The rest of the mandals accounts for a very low ratio of the Scheduled Tribe population. The Scheduled Tribes comprise chiefly Chenchus, Yerukulas, Lambadas, Yanadis and Koyas who live in the forest and remote areas in the district. But they come under the category of caste Hindus. The Chenchus are mostly found in Pargi, Doma, Kulkacherla, Chevella and Maheshwaram

Mandals, while the Lambadas and Naiks live in Dharur, Bashirabad, Tandur and Peddamul Mandals. The tribal population is mostly engaged as agriculture labourers and during the non-agriculture season, they work as stone cutters in the railway line areas and sell fire wood in urban areas.

The tribal Ahram Patashhala (Ahram schools) are located at Banda Elka Cherla and Regundi villages, under the Integrated Tribal Development Project. A Chenchu colony near Enkepally popularly known as "Chaitanya Nagar" has come up for the upliftment of the Tribal population. The District Co-operative Society and Tribal Development Agency is rendering services for the betterment of the tribal community.[1]

Table 2.9: Scheduled Tribe Population

Sl. No.		Andhra Pradesh	Ranga Reddy district
1.	1971: Total	535.50	158.21
	1981: Total	663.53	255.20
2.	1981: STs	31.76	72.50
	1991: STs	63.00	10.09
3.	1981: Growth of (%)	23.82	42.60
	1991: Growth of (%)	50.00	61.30
4.	1981: Growth of STs (%)	5.90	6.00
	1991: Growth of STs (%)	9.50	5.50

Source: Andhra Pradesh Year Book 1993, Data News Feature Publication, Hyderabad

Literacy

There are 10,61,109 literates in the district and the literacy rate in the district is about 42.2 per cent as per the 1991 Census as against 29.7 per cent in 1981. In the district as a whole, mandals such as Vallabhnagar, Rajendranagar Mandal, Pargi, Ibrahimpatnam, Vikarabad, Chevella, Shankarpally, Tandur, Kukatpally, Shabad, Nawabpet, Maheshwaram have literacy rates lower than the regional average.

Table 2.10: Literacy Percentage of AP and Ranga Reddy District

Sl. No.	Year	Andhra Pradesh	Ranga Reddy District
1.	1981	19.28	29.70
2.	1991	45.40	42.20

Source: Hand Book of Statistics of Ranga Reddy District, 1993-94

Tables 2.10 and 2.11 indicate the percentage of literacy in the district.

Table 2.11: Literacy Percentage of Mandal Praja Parishads in Ranga Reddy District (Mandal-wise)

Sl. No.	Name of Mandal	Male	Female	Total	1981%	1991%
1.	Tandur	6089	2270	8319	15.40	21.98
2.	Vikarabad	4066	2845	6911	29.20	40.08
3.	Marpally	6017	1801	7880	14.70	19.11
4.	Mominpet	5984	4874	1858	18.80	29.37
5.	Dharur	5895	1984	7879	15.00	22.02
6.	Peddemul	6044	2126	8170	14.30	19.60
7.	Bashirabad	5568	2012	7580	18.70	21.72
8.	Yalal	4647	1701	6348	14.30	18.73
9.	Bantwaram	4431	1403	5834	14.50	19.72
10.	Nawabpet	1640	1655	3345	19.10	26.03
11.	Pudur	6309	2115	8424	17.80	22.02
12.	Saroornagar	26679	15616	42295	62.90	68.02
13.	Qutballapur	6591	2515	9150	27.30	32.48
14.	Medchal	11590	5857	17477	28.20	37.46
15.	Maheshwaram	8340	3233	11573	15.70	24.69
16.	Manchal	7214	2533	9737	20.70	26.23
17.	Kesara	6139	2655	8794	37.70	42.31
18.	Ibrahimpatnam	12904	5598	18502	24.20	31.97
19.	Kandukur	7361	2702	10063	18.70	22.64
20.	Yacharam	8658	3241	11899	20.50	27.22
21.	Shamirpet	12195	5469	17664	20.30	31.08
22.	Ghatkeser	12613	6447	19060	30.40	42.37
23.	Hayatnagar	13716	5058	18774	36.70	40.49
24.	Chevella	9445	2669	12114	18.90	24.25
25.	Pargi	6409	2115	8424	19.90	24.02
26.	Rajendernagar	7870	4167	12037	38.90	47.69
27.	Doma	4811	1374	6185	12.60	17.46
28.	Gandeed	7258	2618	9876	16.40	20.02
29.	Shamshabad	11946	5142	17088	27.80	28.65
30.	Shankerpally	10317	3876	14246	22.90	28.44
31.	Kulkacherla	5576	1833	7409	11.60	15.91
32.	Moinabad	8823	3188	12011	19.50	26.21
33.	Shabad	7756	2877	10633	18.70	24.52

Source: Zilla Parishad Office, Ranga Reddy district

On the whole, the literacy rate in Ranga Reddy district shows a step rise from 1981 to 1991. However, the literacy rate during 1981 was 20.70 per cent had increased to 42.20 per cent in 1991. From Table 12.11, it is also observed that the male population dominates the female in literacy rate. The mandals nearer to Hyderabad city such as Saroonnagar, Medchal, Ibrahimpatnam, Shamirpet, Ghatkesar, Hayatnagar, Shamshabad and Shankerpally in Ranga Reddy district have achieved more literacy rates when compared to other mandals because of their nearness to Hyderabad city and more exposure to educational atmosphere as well. On the whole, the Ranga Reddy district has a larger number of literates both among male and female population.

Town Municipalities in the District

In the district, the population covered by sixteen township areas has more than 6.00 lakh as against 2,83,223 population as per the 1981 Census. The sixteen township areas are (1) Alwal, (2) Balanagar, (3) Bowenpally, (4) Budwel, (5) Fathenagar, (6) Ghatkesar, (7) Kapra, (8) Kukatpally, (9) Macha Bolaram, (10) Moosapet, (11) Qutbullapur, (12) Vikarabad, (13) Tandur, (14) Shamhabad, (15) Yapral and (16) Malkajgiri.

There are eleven municipalities in Ranga Reddy district, in which two municipalities, namely, Tandur and Vikarabad are located in Vikarabad division. They are (1) Kapra, (2) Malkajgiri, (3) L.B. Nagar, (4) Rajendranagar, (5) Kukatpally, (6) Alwal, (7) Uppal, (8) Vikarabad, (9) Kutubullapur, (10) Sherlingampally, (11) Tandur. It is interesting to note that Tandur which is the border taluka touching the Karnataka border of Chincholi is one of the most important commercial centres.

Parliament and Assembly Constituencies

The district has no Lok Sabha constituency. There are six Assembly segments within the district, namely (1) Chevella, (2) Pargi, (3) Vikarabad, (4) Tandur, (5) Ibrahimpatnam, (6) Medchel. One is reserved for Scheduled Caste and there are five general constituencies.

Land Utilisation

As indicated earlier, the total geographical area of the district is 7,47,726 lakh hectares of which 68,574 lakh hectares are covered by forest, 42,382 lakh hectares are in the category of barren and uncultivable land. The land put to non-agricultural use is around 85,748 lakhs hectares. A total area of 45,705 thousand hectares is utilized as permanent pasture and other grazing lands. The area under miscellaneous tree crop and groves not included in net area sown is around 7,335 hectares. The cultivable wasteland is 26,471 lakh hectares, the other fallow land are in the range of 61,590 lakh hectares, while current fallow lands are in the range of 1,17,498 lakh hectares. The net area sown is of the order of 2,93,423 lakh hectares. The data is presented in Table 2.12.

Table 2.12: Land Utilisation of the District: 1994-95 to 1996-97

Sl.No.	Land Utilisation	1994-95	1995-96	1996-97
1.	Geographical area	247,726	747,726	747,726
2.	Forest	70,066	69,963	68,574
3.	Barren & uncultivable land	42,476	42,014	42,382
4.	Land put to non-agriculture use	84,709	85,618	85,748
5.	Permanent postures & other grazing lands	50,458	49,448	45,705
6.	Miscellaneous tree crops & Grooves not included in net area	7,780	7,354	7,335
7.	Cultivable waste	27,376	27,007	26,471
8.	Other fallow lands	56,742	58,184	61,590
9.	Current fallow lands	118,157	106,920	117,498
10.	Net Area sown	289,018	301,718	292,423

Source: *Hand Book of Statistics of Ranga Reddy District, 1983-84 & 1990-91, AP Year Book 1993*, Data Features, Hyderabad

Area Under Irrigation

Gross irrigated area in the district is 1,11,455 acres which form 15.41 per cent of the gross cropped area. The irrigation facilities in the district are not so rich when compared with other neighbouring districts like Medak, Nalgonda and Mahabubnagar. The variation in the fertility of soils accounts for the difference in the cropping pattern of the eastern and western regions in the district, while sandy lands occur in the eastern region, namely Hayatnagar and Ibrahimpatnam, while the black cotton soil predominate in the western region, namely Chevella, Pargi, Vikarabad and Tandur. Though two good potential rivers flow in the district, there are no irrigation projects. River Musi runs through the district which is untapped for irrigation as feeds Himayatnagar and Osmanagar lakes which supply drinking water to the metropolis. However, the sources of irrigation are mostly tanks, tube wells and canals. The area irrigated through canals during kharif and rabi seasons in 1994-95, stretches over 1,018 hectares, while tanks irrigate 2,094 hectares. Tube wells similarly provide irrigation facility to the tune of 19,867 hectares. The other sources tapped for irrigating lands stretch over 1,532 hectares. The net irrigated area during 1994-95 was around 44,781 hectares while the area irrigated more than once stretches over 15,378 hectares. The gross irrigated area is 60,206 hectares. A comparative picture of the area irrigated through different sources year-wise in the last five years (1991-91 to 1994-95) is presented in Table 2.13.

Table 2.13: Year-wise Source of Area Irrigated (Hectares)

Sl.No.	Source of Irrigation	1990-91	1991-92	1992-93	1993-94	1994-95
1.	Canals	3,743	3,466	2,312	22,227	1,018
2.	Tanks	16,624	14,884	68,574	3,220	2,094
3.	Tube wells	7,560	8,814	5,182	17,228	19,867
4.	Other sources	3,929	3,868	12,478	3,303	1,532
5.	Net area irrigated	634,922	69,540	51,227	44,596	44,781
6.	Area irrigated more than once	—	—	18,647	19,804	15,378
7.	Gross area irrigated	86,919	90,477	69,874	64,401	60,206

Source: Hand Book of Statistics of Ranga Reddy District, 1983-84 & 1990-91, *AP Year Book*, 1993, Data Features, Hyderabad.

In the data collected from the district headquarters, it is found that paddy, jowar, bajra, ragi, greengram, horsegram, redgram, sesamum, castor, cotton, coriander and other crops are produced. The total cropped area during 1994-95 stretched over 1,11,455 hectares. A comparative picture of the area under principal crops, year-wise from 1990-91 to 1994-95 is presented in Table 2.14.

Table 2.14: Area under Principal Crops Year-wise 1990-91 to 1994-95

Sl. No.	Crops	1989-90	1991-92	1992-93	1993-94	1994-95
1.	Rice	135,731	148,218	107,662	96,505	34,331
2.	Jowar	254,784	255,584	249,374	237,400	91,671
3.	Bajra	5,491	4,059	4,278	4,141	9,344
4.	Ragi	20,036	21,496	21,000	28,372	9,444
5.	Greengram	28,234	28,952	36,557	35,382	16,421
6.	Horsegram	5,254	4,972	7,532	6,812	3,149
7.	Redgram	16,468	70,849	68,472	58,441	27,330
8.	Blackgram	19,760	17,590	22,243	24,509	9,714
9.	Groundnut	5,333	22,103	19,324	20,436	5,127
10.	Sesamum	61,309	4,876	5,002	4,894	2,034
11.	Castor	7,483	62,441	56,489	65,997	27,077
12.	Sunflower	9,031	1,670	9,446	22,977	5,088
13.	Chillies		8,816	8,799	8,087	3,128
14.	Cotton	—	—	—	—	—
15.	Wheat	5,695	5,382	4,257	3,933	—
16.	Maize	10,140	70,849	9,292	—	4,814
17.	Coriender	2,230	1,735	1,711	1,797	452

Source: Planning and Statistics Dept, Ranga Reddy district

The following are the average yields of different crops in normal years presented in Table 2.15.

Table 2.15: Average Yield Per Hectare

Sl. No.	Crops	Yield per acre in kgs.
1.	Paddy (irrigated)	22,350
2.	Jowar	870
3.	Bajra	385
4.	Chillies	770
5.	Ragi	1,299
6.	Horse gram	302
7.	Redgram	468
8.	Groundnut	83
9.	Castor	292
10.	Wheat	410

Source: Chief Planning Officer, Ranga Reddy district

Forests

The total forest area in the district is 68,574 hectares. The district cannot boost of any important timber yielding forest because of the low rainfall and inhospitable soil conditions. A total of 1.90 lakh hectares are covered by the forest of which Vikarabad division comprises 40 hectares, while Chevella division has 60 hectares. Eucalyptus is mostly produced in Vikarabad. The fire wood is produced both in Chevella and Vikarabad. The inferior type of forest yielding only thorn, fuel and small timber which the soil can sustain is found in the eastern portion of the district, while the forests are mostly restricted to isolated hills while in the western portion.

Table 2.16: Educational Institutions: 1995-96

Sl. No.	Institutions	No. of Institutions
1.	Primary Schools	1,184
2.	Upper Primary Schools	297
3.	Secondary Schools	323
4.	Junior Colleges	70
5.	Degree Colleges	22
6.	PG Centres	10
7.	ITIs	3
8.	Polytechnic colleges	1
9.	College of Educations	2
10.	TTI (DIET)	1
11.	Law Colleges	3
12.	Agricultural Colleges	2

Source: Gazetted Administrative Officer of District Education, Ranga Reddy district

Education

In the field of education, the district is very backward due to the dominance of Muslim-rule. The Nizam of Hyderabad did not give any importance for the expansion of education in the Atraf-E-Balda district. The Panchayati Raj administration however played an important role in opening primary schools in almost all the rural areas of the district. During the last three decades, a number of educational institutions have come up in the district. As per the 1995 records, there are 1704 schools among which 1184 are primary schools, 297 upper primary schools and 323 are secondary schools. Besides the above, there are as many as 70 junior colleges, 22 Degree colleges and 10 PG colleges catering to the needs of the students of higher education. The technical institutions include ITI, Polytechnic colleges, colleges of education, ITI (DIET) and Law colleges. Altogether, there are 1818 educational institutional at all the levels. All these institutions accommodate around 5.2 lakhs students and around 6200 teachers. The number of educational institutions is shown Table 2.16.

Transport and Communication

The District Head quarters, i.e. Hyderabad, is totally connected with all the Mandals, and Tandur, Morpelly, Vikarabad, Shamshabad and Medchal Mandals are also connected by road and railways.

There are 18 broad guage and 16 meter-guage railway stations in the district with 191.12 kms of broad guage and 186.25 kms meter guage of narrow guage. The Bombay, Rayalaseema, Bangalore Minar, Manjeeva are the important express trains passing through the district. As regards the motor vehicles on the road, it may be mentioned that there are 558 heavy vehicles, while light vehicles are around 3,462. The A.P. Road Transport Corporation is playing a predominant role in providing better transport facilities in Ranga Reddy district, specially in rural areas. There are six Bus Depots in the district, viz. Hyderabad unit I, Hyderabad unit II, Picket, Medchel, Tandur and Pargi.

The number of motor vehicles and railway tracks is indicated in Table 2.17.

Table 2.17: Transport and Communication 1994-95

Sl. No.	Item	Length in kms
	A. Railway Track	
1.	(a) Broad Guage	191.12
2.	(b) Meter Guage	186.25
3.	(c) Narrow Guage	9.00
	B. Motor Vehicles on Road	
4.	(a) Heavy Vehicles	558
5.	(b) Light Vehicles	3,462

Source: Zilla Parishad Office, Ranga Reddy district

Table 2.18: Length of Roads in the District as on 31.3.1995

(kms)

Item	Black top	Metalled	Upmetalled	Total
National Highway				
State (PWD):				
(a) State Highways	148.00	—	—	148.00
(b) Major District Roads	320.522	28.013	—	348.54
(c) Other District Roads	56.94	35.95	—	92.89
Zilla Paraja Parishad:				
(a) Major District Roads	242.09	855.21	383.15	1480.45
(b) Other District Roads	—	—	—	
(c) Village Roads	—	—	—	
Mandal Praja Parishad	23.70	503.63	1192.10	1719.43
Total	791.252	1422.803	1575.250	3789.305

Source: *Ibid*.

Civil Supplies

In order to ensure proper distribution of essential commodities among the people, more particularly the weaker sections, there are altogether 1334 fair price shops in the district, among them, 968 are located in rural areas and 366 in urban areas. The State Government has provided White cards to 1,25,219 households and Pink cards to 1,85,559 households. All essential commodities like rice, wheat, kerosene, sugar, palm oil are distributed through these fair price shops on the basis of the category of the ration cards and quota supplies. The details are shown in Table 2.19.

Table 2.19: Public Distribution System in Ranga Reddy District as on 23.10.1997

No. of Fair Price Shops	White Cards	Pink Cards	Total

Source: *Ibid*.

Rice Procurement

There has been a steep fall in paddy production in the district during 1996-97 which is borne out from the fact that civil supplies department could procure only 54,946 metric tonne during the year due to the steep fall in production. The comparative figures are given in Table 2.20.

Table 2.20: Rice Procurement 1996-97

(Mt. tonnes)

Sl. No.	Year	Rice Procurement by FCI	Sold outside	Total	Paddy brought out from outside
1.	1994-95	53,664	50582.00	104,246	70,740
2.	1995-96	46,606	40550.00	87,156	31,320
3.	1996-97	54,946	7946.00	62,892	63,780

Source: District Civil Supplying Officer, Ranga Reddy district

Tourism

There are a few historical places which are significant from the viewpoint of tourism in the district. Among such tourist centers, mention may be made of the Ananthagiri Hills center, which is 5 km away from the Vikarabad erstwhile block. It is not only a place of tourism but a picnic spot also.

Table 2.21: Particulars of Tourist Centre

Sl.No.	Place of Tourist Centre	Erstwhile Block	Distance from		Mode of Transport	Travellers Bungalow Chowltry	Important festival days
			Block H.Qrs. kms.	Dist. H.Qrs. kms.			
1.	Ananthagiri	Vikarabad	5	90	Bus	I.V.	—
2.	Rangapur					Sanitorium	
3.	Observatory	Ibrahimpatnam	4	80	Bus		
4.	Deep Park	Shameerpet	1	25	Bus		
5.	Deer Park	Hyatnagar	5	25	Bus		
6.	Hym...	Rajendranagar	8	25	Bus	Tr. Bunglow	
7.	Kisargutta	Kisar	8	40	Bus	Tr. Bunglow	Shivaratri
8.	Lord Shiva Temple	Maheshwaram	1	36	Bus	Shivaratri	
9.	Sita Rama	Chevella	1	45	Bus		Sri Rama Navami

Source: Office of the Collector, Ranga Reddy district

Rangapur observatory complex is also famous. This place is 4 km away from Ibrahimpatnam. Shameerpet is only a small village about 30 years old but on account of the devotion of a single soul it has attained importance. Another place of interest is the Deer Park which is situated 5 km away from erstwhile Hayatnagar Mandal. The Himayatsagar lake is also famous. This lake provides drinking water to the Hyderabad citizens. It is not only a place of tourism but a picnic spot as well. The Kisaragutta temple is also famous. It is otherwise famous as Kisara Shivlayam, the annual jathara (Shivaratri) taking place during the month of March. Another tourist attraction is Lord Shiva Temple. This place is one km away from Maheshwaram Mandal. Another place of interest is Sita Ram Devastanam which is situated one km away from erstwhile Chevella Mandal headquarters. The above data clearly showed in Table 2.21.

Table 2.22: Medical and Health Facilities as on 31.3.1995

Sl. No. Particulars	1994-95
I Allopathic:	
1. Hqrs. Hospital for Special Treatment	14
2. Civil Hospitals:	-
(a) Government dispensaries	-
3. Primary Health Centres:	-
(a) Old P.H.Cs.	34
(b) Mandal P.H.Cs.	12
(c) New P.H.Cs.	6
4. Leprosy Control Units	-
5. Mobile Medical Units	-
6. T.B. Centres and Dispensaries	-
7. Doctors	1
8. Doctors per lakh of population	73
9. Beds	5
10. No. of beds per lakh of population	418
II Ayurvedic:	
1. Dispensaries	12
2. Doctors/Vaids	12
III Unani:	
1. Dispensaries	14
2. Doctors/Vaids	14
IV Homeopathy:	
1. Dispensaries	7
2. Doctors/Vaids	7

Source: District Medical and Health Department, Ranga Reddy district

Medical and Health

In order to provide better medical aid to the rural population, there are 34 old primary health centres, 12 Mandal primary health Centres, six Mandal level new primary health centres, four additional health centres and 14 Government Civil Hospitals. In recent years, the State Government upgraded Medchal, Pargi and Vikarabad civil hospitals into 30 bedded hospitals, T.B. Centres and dispensaries. Altogether 73 doctors attend to the patients. This district has a total bed capacity of 418. On an average, five doctors are available for every one lakh of population and 10 beds are available for one lakh of population. Besides, the above Allopathic medical centres, there are Ayurveda, Unani, Homeopathy centres also. In the case of Ayurveda treatment, there are 12 dispensaries and 12 doctors/Vaidya. Similarly, in the case of Unani, there are 14 dispensaries and 14 doctors/Tabeebs. Homeopathic treatment is also provided through seven dispensaries, which have altogether seven physicians. The data in this regard is presented in Table 2.22.

Table 2.23: Animal Husbandry and Veterinary Services 1995-96

Sl. No.	Particulars	1994-95
1.	No. of ISS Units by VAS	45
2.	No. of Veterinary Hospitals	9
3.	No. of Livestock Supervisory Units	52
4.	No. of Rural Livestock Units	145
5.	No. of RLS Units by Vet. Assts.	70
6.	No. of Animal Health Centre	1
7.	No. of Mobile Input Projects	1
8.	No. of Calves Born	12,389
9.	Geo.	4,115
10.	Indigenous	11
11.	Murrah	8,263
12.	No. of artificial.....	32,771
13.	Geo.	11,315
14.	Indigenous	37
15.	Murrah	21,419

Source: Joint Director, Animal Husbandry, Ranga Reddy district

In the beginning of the 20th century, when medical aid and the doctors were not available to save the lives of the poor patients and after witnessing the deplorable health conditions of the rural masses in Vikarabad division, medical hospital was established, which is today serving the needs of the rural people with X-ray and maternity facilities.

Animal Husbandry

The data relating to animal husbandry and veterinary services during the year 1995 is provided in Table 2.23.

Power Consumption

The details in regard to power consumption in the year 1994 under different categories in the district is provided in Table 2.24. The district is provided with different KV lines such as 220 KV, 132 KV, 66 KV, 33 KV, 11 KV and low tension which runs into 14,465.2 kms. It is commendable to point out that cent per cent electrification is provided in the district.

The data concerning transmission and distribution is presented in Table 2.24.

Table 2.24: Growth of Transmission and Distribution Lines 1994-95

(in k.m.)

Sl. No.	Name of the Line	Length 0 in k.ms
1.	220 KV	168
2.	132 KV	376
3.	66 KV	124
4.	33 KV	855
5.	11 KV	3,762
6.	LT (Low tension)	14,466

Source: Office of Divisional Engineer, APSEB, Ranga Reddy district

Table 2.25: Police Station and Police Force 1993-94

Sl.No.	Particulars	As on 31.3.1994
1.	No. of Police Stations	44 (including)
2.	No. of Outposts	
3.	Police Force:	
	Ordinary (Civil):	
	(a) Officers (CI)	26
	SIs	92
	(b) Head Constables	274
	(c) ASIs	29
	(d) Police Constables	1,255

Police and Crime

The number of police stations and police forces by the end of 1993 in Ranga Reddy district is provided in Table 2.25. The incidence of crime in the district as on 31.3.1994 illustrates the fact that the crime rate is low when compared to other districts of AP in general and Rayalseema in particular.

Table 2.26: Incidence of Crime 1990-91 of Ranga Reddy District

Sl.No.	Particulars	As on 31.3.1994
1.	Murders	103
2.	Dacoity	20
3.	Robbery	58
4.	House Breaking Day & Night	98
5.	Cattle thefts	71
6.	Ordinary thefts	606
7.	Others	190

Source: Superintendent of Police, Ranga Reddy district

Social Welfare

The State Government of Andhra Pradesh has provided social welfare services/institutions such as social welfare hostels, tribal welfare hostels, tribal welfare ashram schools, special nutrition programme for tribals, backward classes hostels, etc. There are altogether 71 social welfare hostels for Scheduled Castes accommodating more than 7,000 boys. Similarly, there are 13 girls' hostels, which accommodate around 1,000 girls as boarders. These hostels by and large are spread over almost all mandals within the district. Tribal welfare hostels are provided for both for boys and girls located in 45 mandals. There are 44 boys and 15 girls hostels. Similarly, there are tribal welfare ashram schools in the district located at Kisaragutta with 377 boarders. Apart from this, there are 15 Backward Classes Hostels in Ranga Reddy district accommodating 1283 boarders.

Industrial Growth

The level of industrial development in the erstwhile Hyderabad district is comparatively low in spite of the availability of plenty of raw materials. The feudal background of the district might have been responsible for the non-existence of enterprise. However, Ranga Reddy district has been surrounded by the largest number of agro-based industries. The district ranks first in respect of chemical and allied industries in the State. The A.P. Industrial Infrastructure Development Corporation had established industrial estates and industrial development areas at the following centres: (1) Vikarabad, (2) Uppal, (3) Balanagar, (4) Katedan, (5) Kushaiguda, (6) Jeedimatla, (7) Nacharam, (8) Kukatpally and (9) Medchal.

There are nine Central Government public sector projects, 34 large and medium scale industries and 11 projects are under implementation. There are 12060 registered small-scale industrial units working in the district employing about 8,000 persons. But most of the industrial development has taken place in areas around the twin cities. None of the above industrial enterprises could provide employment to the youth belonging to Vikarabad, Tandur, Pargi and Chevella regions. Rural non-agricultural labourers are the major sufferers of poverty and misery due to non-existence of industrial development in the district although there are six public sector and 28 private sector engineering industries in the district. Table 2.27 indicates various industries in the district.

Table 2.27: Small-scale Industrial Units Set Up in the District (1991-92)

Sl. No.	Particulars	No. of Units	₹ in Lakh Investment
1.	Agro based	854	208.88
2.	Food based	—	—
3.	Forest based	—	—
4.	Mineral based	—	—
5.	General Engineering based	2,502	611.40
6.	Paper & Allied Products	—	—
7.	Livestock based	—	—
8.	Electrical & Electronics	—	—
9.	Textile based	—	—
10.	Chemical based	—	—
11.	Others (Miscellaneous)	492	124.02
	Total	3,848	944.30

Source: District Industries Centre, Ranga Reddy district

3

Components of Jawahar Rozgar Yojana

Rural development is a dynamic concept. It assumes significance in the context of socio-political and economic dualism in developing countries and the efforts being made by the National Government to develop the rural masses from poverty and deprivation. The Integrated Rural Development in India has its origin in integrated area development programmes envisaged in the Fourth Five-Year Plan. It is being looked upon as the technology of development for rural India. While economic growth emphasizes maximization of production, rural development focuses integration of function with area.

The recent upsurge of interest in integrated development arises from the realization of the need for accelerating rural development. The rural poor derive enduring benefits from a variety of schemes intended for them. The success of different schemes, under rural development, depend on the inter action among the schemes and also on the structural and institutional environment influencing and conditioning the operation of development schemes. The integrated rural plan meant for the development of the rural poor should, inter, alia, aim at optimizing utilization of resources and existing infrastructure, narrowing the gap between inter-regional and inter-sectoral differences in the rate of growth, bringing about a balance between production and consumption, maximizing and avoiding the evils of urbanization. What is needed in a socio-economic set up like India particularly under the existing conditions is that the state should not only provide resources and entrepreneurship for the launching of social welfare development programmes, but also must monitor, nourish and supervise the execution of its schemes at every stage with a missionary zeal until the objective is achieved.

It is very difficult to give a precise definition of the concept of rural development is very difficult of rural development. In a rich country, rural development would mean preserving and developing the country side with its natural beauty without being polluted by the industrial atmosphere. The rural area would be provided with amenities which perhaps the very rich can afford. In poor countries, rural development would be synonymous with the development of the poor because the rural areas are largely inhabited by poor people. Therefore, rural development is to be understood in terms of contextual concerns.

In India, rural development is generally equated with the development of the rural poor. However, the concept of rural development has two major components, viz. the locational aspect and the living conditions of the inhabitants of the location.[1] The locational aspect takes into consideration the residential facilities, the infrastructural facilities including roads, electricity, piped water, sanitation, educational and health facilities, communication and entertainment facilities and financial institutions.

In most countries, the provision of infrastructural facilities depends on the density of population of an area, the rural and urban classification is based on a cut-off point of a certain number of population within an area. In India, the census definition of a rural area is that the smallest area of rural habitation is the village. It generally follows the limits of a revenue village that is recognized by the district administration. The revenue village may not necessarily be a single conglomeration of habitations. It may have one or more hamlets. But the revenue village has a definite surveyed boundary and each village is a separate administrative unit with separate village accounts. There may be unsurveyed villages within forests where the locally recognized boundaries of each habitation area are followed within a larger unit of the forest range officer's jurisdiction. Hence, the concept of rural development may be defined as the development of infrastructural facilities for the people residing in the area and improving the standard of living of those people. The development of infrastructural facilities depend on the force of demand for such facilities from the people living in the area. It may be noted that the demand of the infrastructural facilities is positively correlated with the incomes of the people. Higher the income of the people grater is the demand for such facilities. Higher income of the people will result in the improvement of their standard of living which can be substantially improved through proper infrastructural facilities.

However, with the improved financial base and new technological approaches to the programmes of rural development over the years, some of the long neglected aspects such as rural women, social welfare problems through non-formal functional education or vocational training, health and family welfare education, etc. have been taken up by the government in selected blocks and districts of the state. The identification and selection of beneficiaries of the target group in an area, fixation of plan targets, allocation of resources and personnel for each programme, etc. are all done on the same lines of developmental planning, keeping in view the socio-economic conditions of the selected families, resource availability, and the extent to which the target group could be exposed to the various programmes of development in each area. But the principal factor to be reckoned with is that the state which has been the motive force behind all these developmental activities for the upliftment of the rural poor over the past few decades, has remained a catalytic agent diverting its responsibilities and depending on its middle and lower order functionaries for formulating and implementing welfare developmental programmes, not much concerned about the end results of such programmes.[2]

In the integrated exercise of planning for social and economic development, co-ordinated measures for an accelerated development programme assumes exceptional significance. The rural administrative bodies have both co-operating and co-ordination roles. In the present set up democratic decentralization, the rural area has a representative structure of government where the administrators, elected leaders and local population participate in the development effort. In fact, the elected representatives play a key role in the decision-making process. Leaders are recognized as facilitators of the process of development.[3] Since the emphasis of rural development policies is bringing about people's participation in the development programmes, it is possible to achieve this through the leaders.[4] The administrators are expected to participate with missionary zeal in the life and development of the villages. And these institutions are to be galvanized to become effective instruments of social and economic change.

Poverty Alleviation

Alleviation of rural poverty has been a major subject of the Seventh Five-Year Plan which aimed at bringing down the percentage of people below the poverty line. The approach paper for the Eighth Plan indicates that this will continue to be the goal during the Eighth Plan also. Since the prevalence of unemployment and under-employment in the rural areas is a contributing factor for high incidence of poverty, the main thrust in achieving the objective of poverty alleviation was directed towards creation of supplementary employment opportunities for the rural poor during the lean agricultural season through various public works programmes. The approaches to the Eighth Plan stress the need for having a sharper focus on programmes aimed at giving self-employment and wage employment to the poorer sections of the community.

Jawahar Rozgar Yojana (JRY)

During the first four years of the Seventh Five-Year Plan, two wage employment programmes, viz. National Rural Employment Programme and Rural Landless Employment Guarantee Programme were in operation in the country. From April 1989 both these programmes were merged into a single rural employment programme known as Jawahar Rozgar Yojana. In the context of the New Economic Policy, it was felt necessary to continue Jawahar Rozgar Yojana as the largest single employment programme in the country during the Eighth Five-Year Plan period. However, on the basis of the experience gained in implementing the wage employment programmes in general and the Jawahar Rozgar Yojana in particular, strategy for implementation of Jawahar Rozgar Yojana was modified from 1993-94 to ensure better implementation of the Yojana during the Eight-Plan, especially to achieve the target of providing substantial days of employment per person in backward districts where there is concentration of unemployed and under-employed persons.

The Objectives of Jawahar Rozgar Yojana

The salient features and objectives of the Yojana Programme are as given below:[5]

(i) Primary objective: Generation of additional gainful employment for the unemployed and under-employed in the rural areas.

(ii) Secondary objective: Creation of sustained employment by strengthening the rural economic infrastructure and assets and improvement in the overall quality of life in the rural areas.

(iii) Expenditure under the programme was to be shared between the centre and the states in the ratio of 80:20.

(iv) Central assistance released to the state. The State Governments are required to release the grants to District Rural Development Authorities/Zilla Parishads within a week after the release of central assistance along with their own matching share.

(v) Six per cent and 20 per cent of the programme resources are earmarked to Jawahar Rozgar Yojana.

(vi) Preference to Scheduled Castes, Scheduled Tribes and freed bonded labourers is to be provided in employment.

(vii) Resources of two or more districts/Village Panchayats can be pooled to take up works for common benefits of the concerned districts/Village Panchayats.

(viii) Thirty per cent of employment opportunities are to be reserved for women.

(ix) In case of Union Territories, entire resources under the Yojana programme will be provided by the Central Government.

(x) Works can be taken up for execution during any part of the year whenever the need for generating employment is felt, preferably during the lean agricultural season and may continue during the busy agricultural period too.

(xi) Two kilograms of food grains per day is given to the workers at subsidized rates and the issue price is 50 paisa per kilogram. Distribution of food grains is through PDS only in the case of ravaged blocks and for others it is either through PDS or at work site as convenient to the State Governments.

(xii) Contractors or middle men are not permitted to be engaged for executing any of the works.

(xiii) At least 60 per cent o the resources have to be spent as wage components.

(xiv) Upto a maximum of 26 per cent of annual allocation allowed to be spent on administrative or contingent expenditure at state, district, village panchayat level. District rural development and zilla parishads can spend upto a maximum of ₹ 50,000 on training of officials, non-officials involved in the implementation of Jawahar Rozgar Yojana at the district and village panchayat level.

(xv) A maximum of 10 per cent of the annual allocation can be used for incurring expenditure on maintenance of such assets which have not been taken over by a department of the State Government.

Works under the Jawahar Rozjar Yojana

Government of India has also provided an illustrative list of works, which could be taken up under the programe.[6] All rural works which result in creation of durable productive community assets can be taken up under the Yojana. It has been mentioned that preference is to be given to the following works:

(i) Having potential of maximum direct and continuing benefits to the members of poverty groups, who in the normal course, would have been left out of the process of development; and

(ii) Works which are owned by or are assigned to such groups of beneficiaries either for direct use of the assets by the groups or for sale of the facilities created by the assets to ensure continuing income to the groups.

It is also mentioned that priority may also be given to works which are required for providing infrastructure for other poverty alleviation programmes like IRDP, DWCRA, DPAP, DDP and construction of primary school buildings in those revenue village which have primary schools without buildings. While utilizing funds for providing infrastructure support, the ratio between wage and material component of 60:40 may be observed. In case there is need for supplementary requirement of funds for material components, it may be provided by dovetailing resources available from other relevant government plan or non-plan programmes. The supplementary requirement of material component may also be provided by dovetailing funds by drawing on own funds of panchayats, cooperatives, other public bodies and community contribution. Illustrative list of the activities for which Yojana resources can be used to provide infrastructure support are as follows:

(i) Planting of mulberry trees;

(ii) Establishment of nurseries;

(iii) Chawki rearing sheds and reeling sheds for seri-culture;

(iv) Poultry sheds;
(v) Handloom sheds;
(vi) Worksheds for agro-processing;
(vii) Retail outlets of district supply and marketing society;
(viii) Raw materials godown and common worksheds for DWCRA group.

Social Forestry and Agri-horticulture Work

The main objective in the implementation of social forestry and agri-horticulture works under JRY is to ensure that its benefits accrue to the rural communities and more particularly to the rural poor. These works also include soil and water conservation measures taken to ensure the survival of the plants. Social forestry and agri-horticulture works under Jawahar Rozgar Yojana may be taken up on government and community lands. If suitable community lands are not available, such works may also be undertaken on degraded forest lands and the entire produce from such lands is made available for the community use under a general or specific order of the State Government. Planting of all types of fruit, fodder and fuel trees can be taken up under the programme. However, the plant species should be selected by the District Rural Development Authorities or Village Panchayats taking into account the need of the area and the agro-climatic conditions. Quick growing fuel, fodder and small timber trees along with the fruit trees of local variety may be given preference over the exotic species. Farmers, particularly the small and marginal farmers below the poverty line should be encouraged to raise nurseries in their own fields or backyards. The benefits of social forestry can directly accrue to the rural poor through the scheme of free patta under which the tree planting permit or tree patta holder shall be entitled to usufructs of trees. The usufruct rights under the tree planting permitting tree patta shall include the rights to gather dead branches, etc. carry on tree based activity like bee keeping, silk worm rearing, lac production, etc. cropping of trees, hypothecate the trees to financial institutions for loans by deposit of tree planting permit or tree patta the financial institution and devolution of the tree planting permit patta on death of the patta holder. The cost of saplings to be planted and the wages for the labour put in by the tree permit or tree patta holder in planting the saplings and also the cost of maintenance of such plantation upto the time the trees are able to survive may be met from the JRY funds.

Farm Forestry and Agri-horticulture

Farm forestry and agri-horticulture may be taken up under JRY only on lands belonging to the following categories of identified rural poor whose names figure in the Integrated Rural Development Programme Survey register.

(i) Scheduled Castes and Scheduled Tribes;

(ii) Freed bonded labourers; and

(iii) All allottees of land whose land holdings do not exceed those of small farmers, and on land for which tree patta has been granted.

Wherever tree plantation has been taken up under the above programme on community land and for community benefits, the cost of maintenance of such plantation upto the time the trees are able to survive or upto the period of three year from the year of plantation, whichever is earlier, may be met from JRY funds. Non-governmental organizations may be involved in all activities relating to social forestry from nursery to plantations through the rural poor. Funding for the non-governmental organization may be done directly by the State Governments or through the District Rural Development Authorities.

Beneficiary-oriented Individual Programmes for Economically Weaker Sections Including Scheduled Castes and Scheduled Tribes

Under JRY programme works can be taken up for the benefit of identified individuals below the poverty line. The illustrative list of such works is as below:

(i) Construction of houses for individuals along with development of infrastructure facilities.

(ii) Development of allotted land in the case of allottees of ceiling surplus land, bhoodan land, government land whether they belong to Scheduled Castes or Scheduled Tribes category or not.

(iii) Social forestry works such as fuel-wood and fodder plantations and agri-horticulture on the private lands belonging to the target groups.

(iv) Minor irrigation wells and groups wells.

(v) Drinking water wells.

Provision for Land Development of Small or Marginal Farmers Below Poverty Line and Formulation of Land Development Project

It is significant to note that the private land belonging to small and marginal farmers who are below poverty line and figure in Integrated Rural Development Programme register can be developed with JRY funds. Land shaping, construction of drainage, field channels, etc. are the items of work which will constitute land development. All capital expenditure on land development including the costs of soil and irrigation will be permissible under land development subject to the condition that not less than 60 per cent expenditure of a land development project will be incurred on payment of wages to unskilled labourers at the level of an implementing agency. Dovetisling of resources from other sources will be permissible to make up for excess material component of land development project. The cost of family labour used for cultivation of developed land will also be permissible to small and marginal farmers below the poverty line whose names figure in Integrated Rural Development Programme survey register for maximum period of two years only at the rate of 100 mandays per year calculated at minimum wages for unskilled labour. Recurring costs of cultivation on items like seeds, chemical fertilizers, insecticides, pesticides, weedicides, irrigation, etc. will not be permissible under a land development project even if it forms parts of a project. Any project capable of improving the productivity of land in a watershed or command area will be treated as a land development project. Only such blocks of land would be permitted under Jawahar Rozgar Yojana which have atleast ten farmers, and at least 50 per cent of the land holders who are small and marginal farmers and at least 25 per cent of the land belongs to small and marginal farmers. No recovery of the cost of land development will be made from the small and marginal farmers. In the case of big farmers, recovery will be made by the Village Panchayat at the rate prescribed by the State Government.

Food Grains Distribution Under Jawahar Rozgar Yojana Programme

Distribution of food grains as part of wages under rural employment programmes is based on the principles of protecting the real wages of the workers besides improving the national standards of the families of the rural poor. Food grains should be given as part of wages under JRY in view of its sustained benefits to the rural poor at the rate of two kgs per man-day. If the food grains are available in the open market at prices cheaper than those prescribed under the Public Distribution System, the workers engaged under JRY will be at a disadvantage, if food grains are compulsorily given to them at the rates prescribed under Public Distribution System. In view of this possibility, which may occur during some months in a year, distribution of food grains under JRY may be optional depending upon the prices in the open market. The foodgrains for the Yojana will be released to the states generally in instalments along with the release of the JRY resources. The distribution of food grains under the Yojana will be through Public Distribution System only and District Rural Development Authorities or Zilla Parishads will make necessary all arrangements for its distribution among the Village Panchayats or implementing agencies for use on Jawahar Rozgar Yojana Works on cash and carry basis through Public Distribution System shops. If for any reason, the Public Distribution System network cannot be used for distribution of food grains to the workers, the District Rural Development Authorities (DRDAs) or Zilla Parishads may arrange to distribute food grains to the workers engaged under

JRY by actual distribution at the work site. It would be responsibility of the District Rural Development Authorities or Zilla Parishads to ensure that the quality of wheat or rice supplied to them conformed to fair average quality. The concerned officers of the DRDAs or Zilla Parishads should conduct inspection of the stocks before taking delivery of the foodgrains to ensure that food grains below average quality are not accepted. The price of the food grains for distribution to the workers under JRY shall be the same as the price under Public Distribution System in a particular block. Sales tax or any other local tax, if levied by any of the states on food grains supplied by the Food Corporation of India for Jawahar Rozgar Yojana will be borne by the State Government concerned and shall not be charged to the JRY funds.

Indira Awaas Yojana

Indira Awaas Yojana which was launched during 1985-86 as a sub-scheme of Rural Landless Employment Guarantee Programme is being continued as a sub-scheme of Jawahar Rozgar Yojana since its launching from April, 1989. The paramount objective of the Indira Awaas Yojana is primarily to provide houses to members of Scheduled Castes or Scheduled Tribes, freed bonded labourers in rural areas and also to non-Scheduled Castes and to non-Scheduled Tribes among the rural poor who are below the poverty line. The houses under this Yojana will be provided free of cost. From the year 1993-94, 10 per cent of the resources at the national or state level has been earmarked for Indira Awaas Yojana. The funds under this Yojana will be distributed among the districts on the basis of number of rural Scheduled Castes or Scheduled Tribes in a district. Indira Awaas Yojana funds will be operated by District Rural Development Authorities or Zilla Parishads at the district level. The order of priority for selection of beneficiaries amongst target groups is as follows:

- (i) Freed bonded labourers;
- (ii) SC/ST households who are victims of atrocities;
- (iii) SC/ST households, below poverty line, headed by widows and unmarried women;

(iv) SC/ST households affected by flood, fire, earthquake and similar natural calamities;

(v) Other SC/ST households below poverty line; and

(vi) Non-SC/ST households below poverty line.

The allotment of houses under this Yojana will be in the name of the female member of the beneficiary household and it can also be allotted in the joint names of both husband and wife.[7] The houses under Indira Awaas Yojana will be built on individual plots in the main habitation of the village. The houses can also be built on micro habitat approach or in a cluster within a habitation, so as to facilitate the development of infrastructure such as internal roads, drains, drinking water supply, etc. and other common facilities. The implementing agency should always take care to see that the houses under Indira Awaas Yojna are located close to the village and not far away so as the ensure safety and security, nearness to work place and social communication.

Cost of Houses Under Indira Awaas Yojana

Taking into account the increase in the price levels, the cost ceiling for each house has been revised with effect from 1-1-1994. The cost of houses are given in Table 3.1.

Table 3.1: Revised Cost Ceiling for Each House Under Indira Awaas Yojana

Sl.No.	Item	Plain Area	Hill/Difficult Area
		₹	₹
1.	Construction house (basic cost)	9,000	10,800
2.	Construction of latrine and somless chullah	1,500	1,500
3.	Cost of providing infracture and common facilities	3,500	3,500
	Total	14,000	15,800

Source: Government of India, *JRY-Manual for Villages*, Department of Rural Development, New Delhi, June, 1991.

From the above table it has been observed that there is a slight variation in the cost ceiling for each house in plain area and hill or difficult area. It is also mentioned in the manual that in case the houses are not built in clusters or by using the microhabitat approach, then ₹ 3,500/- mentioned in the above

Table 3.1 to provide for infrastructure and common facilities can also be used in the construction of houses. The layout, size, and type design of the house will depend on the local conditions. Hence, no type design is prescribed for Indira Awaas Yojana except that the plinth area of the houses should be around 20 sq.m. The houses should be designed in accordance with the desire of the beneficiaries keeping in view the climatic conditions and the need to provide proper space, kitchen, ventilation, sanitary facilities, smokeless chullah, etc. and also keeping in view the community perceptions, preferences and cultural attitude of the beneficiaries. It is also maintained that no type design should be imposed on the beneficiary and at the same time the cost limits will also have to be kept in view.

The construction of the houses should be done by the beneficiaries themselves from the very beginning. The beneficiaries may make their own arrangement for the construction and may engage skilled workmen on their own and may also contribute family labour. The beneficiaries will have complete freedom as to the manner of construction of the house which is their own. This will result in economy in cost, ensure quality of construction and lead to satisfaction on the part of beneficiaries and acceptance of the house. The responsibility for the proper construction of the house will thus be on the beneficiaries themselves. No contractor is allowed in the construction of Indira Awaas Yojana houses. If any case of construction through contractors comes to notice, Government of India will recover the allocation made to the state for those Indira Awaas Yojana houses. The houses should not also be constructed by the government departments. Government departments or organizations can give technical assistance or arrange for coordinated supply of raw materials such as cement, steel or bricks. A committee of the beneficiaries should be formed to coordinate the work and they should be consulted in all matters relating to Indira Awaas Yojana. Suitable voluntary agencies in the local area with proven good track record wherever available should be associated with the construction of Indira Awaas Yojana houses. These voluntary agencies must be made use of to popularize the use of sanitary latrine and also in the construction of smokeless chullahs.

Million Wells Scheme

Million Wells Scheme was launched as a sub-scheme of National Rural Employment Programme or Rural Landless Employment Guarantee Programme during the year 1988-89 and has since continued during 1989-90 as a sub-scheme of Jawahar Rozgar Yojana. The Million Wells Scheme was launched with the objective of providing open irrigation wells, free of cost, to poor small and marginal farmers belonging to Scheduled Castes, Scheduled Tribes and freed bonded labourers. In view of the importance and significance or Million Wells Scheme in relation to the poor farmers, from the year 1993-94, earmarking of funds for implementation of Million Wells Scheme has been increased from 20 to 30 per cent of the total funds available under Jawahar Rozgar Yojana and its coverage has been extended to include poor, small and marginal farmers belonging to non-Scheduled Caste and non-Scheduled Tribe category also. The Million Wells Scheme is primarily intended for open wells only, and tube wells and bore wells are not to be taken up under this provision. Where wells are not feasible due to geographical factors, the amounts allotted under Million Wells Scheme may be utilized for other schemes of minor irrigation like irrigation tanks, water harvesting structures and also for the development of lands belonging to small and marginal farmers. The amount cannot be diverted for any other schemes.

Owing to geographical reasons, after digging an open well up to some depth, blasting is required to be undertaken because of the hard layer of stones or rock, and thereafter a small bore in required to be drilled to obtain sufficient quantity of water for irrigation purposes. The entire operation may be funded from the scheme provided the outflow from the Million Wells Scheme funds is such that the wage material ratio of 60:40 is maintained at the level of the implementing agency. Where, in a particular financial year, the amount can be spent under Million Wells Scheme only to the extent of 80 per cent of the allocation, the State Government should take up a larger programme so that 100 per cent utilization of allocation of funds in that particular year is possible and the incomplete works are completed during the next financial year within a total period of 12 months from the start of each individual work.

Target group will be small and marginal farmers who are below the poverty line and are listed in the Integrated Rural Development Programme register of the village. While extending benefits under the Scheme, the freed bonded labourers would be given overriding priority. Financial assistance provided to non-Scheduled Caste and non-Scheduled Tribe poor, small and marginal farmers belonging to freed bonded labourers category, under Million Wells Schemes shall not exceed one third of the total funds utilized under Million Wells Scheme in any year.[8]

The order of priority for selection of beneficiaries from different categories of the target group will be as follows:

- (i) Freed bonded labourers;
- (ii) Scheduled Caste/Scheduled Tribe poor, small and marginal farmers who are the victims of authorities;
- (iii) Poor, small and marginal farmers belonging to SC/ST households below poverty line headed by widows and unmarried women;
- (iv) Poor, small and marginal farmers belonging to SC/ST households affected by flood, fire, earthquake and similar natural calamities.
- (v) Poor, small and marginal farmers belonging to other SC/ST house holds below poverty line; and
- (vi) Poor, small and marginal farmers belonging to Non-SC/ST households below poverty line.

The cost and area norms in regard to works under Million Wells Scheme will be decided upon by a committee comprising of Chief Secretary, Secretary (Rural Development), Secretary (Planning), Secretary (Irrigation), and Chief Engineer, Minor Irrigation, of the State. Each well or irrigation source constructed under the scheme will be located in the holding of the beneficiaries and an entry to that effect will be made in the revenue records. The beneficiaries who have already been assisted under Integrated Rural Development Programme for minor irrigation will not be given assistance under this programme. However, there is no bar in providing assistance to those Integrated Rural Development Programme beneficiaries who were not assisted for minor irrigation. The beneficiaries themselves will be asked to undertaken the construction of their wells through their own labour and the local labour for which they will be paid.

Each State Government will constitute a team of officials for each area in its jurisdiction on a district basis to be designated as Certifying Agency for the purpose of certifying failure of wells. Each such team should consist of atleast one technical person, viz. Hydro-geologist or Agricultural Engineer, another government official from the Department of Agriculture or any other department connected with Minor Irrigation Programme. If the District Rural Development Authority comes to the conclusion that a well has failed, it will secure a certificate to that effect from the Certifying Agency. Compensation will be provided to the extent of 100 per cent of the expenditure actually incurred by the farmer towards digging of that well.

There is a possibility under this programme to install a lifting device. The list of the beneficiaries will be passed on to the Project Director of the DRDA so that those intending to install a lifting device may be given preference under Integrated Rural Development Programme and other relevant programmes. The District Collector or Chief Executive Officer of the Zilla Parishad along with the Project Director of the DRDA will be incharge of the monitoring and supervision of the programme in the district. They are also responsible for maintenance of accounts and taking such steps which are essential for speedy implementation of the project. The state level Co-ordination Committee is responsible for state level monitoring. The State Secretary of the Rural Development Department will perform the nodal functions under the scheme.

Criteria and Procedure for Allocation or Release of Resources for Jawahar Rozgar Yojana

The central assistance will be allocated to the states on the basis of proportion of rural poor in a state to the total rural poor in the country. The poverty estimates prepared by the Planning Commission, based on latest available results of National Sample Survey Organisation's survey in this regard will be used for this purpose. The allocation of funds will be made, from the States to the districts, on the basis of index of backwardness formulated on the basis of equal weightage to the proportion of rural Scheduled Caste and Scheduled Tribe population in a district to total Scheduled Caste and Scheduled Tribe population in the State. Not less than 80 per cent of the funds allocated to each district will be distributed to the Village Panchayats which is considered as the lowest level elected body in the district. The balance of 20 per cent of the funds may be utilized at the district level. It is also mentioned that diversion of resources from one district to another district is not permitted in this programme. Similarly, diversion of resources from a Village Panchayat to another village is also not permitted. However, additional allocation can be considered for those district which are performing better and it also depends upon the availability of additional resources. The State Governments have to release their matching share to the District Rural Development Authorities or Zilla Parishads within a week after the release of central assistance. The funds to Village Panchayats will be distributed by the District Rural Development Authorities or Zilla Parishads in accordance with the conditions prescribed in the sanction order of the Government of India. Central assistance will be released every year to the states in two installments. The first installment will be released as soon as the utilization certificate in respect of funds released under first installment in the previous year have been received without any pre-conditions. However, if any specific conditions had been imposed at the time of release of the last installment of the previous year, its compliance will be ensured. The second installment of central funds for the districts will be released by the end of October on the request of the states. The interest amount accrued on the deposits of the Jawahar Rozjar Yojana schemes will be treated as part of the JRY additional resources.

Provision for Maintenance of Assets and Sectoral Earmarking of District Rural Development Authorities or Zilla Parishads Share of Funds

If the District Rural Development Authorities or Zilla Parishads has assets which were created under the erstwhile programmes of NREP/RLEGP or have been created under JRY and have not been taken over by a Department of the State Government, a maximum of 10 per cent of annual allocation can be used for incurring expenditure on maintenance of such assets. District Rural Development Authorities or Zilla Parishads share of 60 per cent funds will be utilized for different sectional works, viz. minor irrigation works, development of rural markets, watershed development projects, social forestry, water and soil conservation measures reclamation of waste lands, nurseries, agri-historiculture, pasture development, link roads selected on the basis of a Master Plan to enhance connectivity of unconnected villages within the district, etc. Around 22.5 per cent of share of funds will be utilized for individual beneficiaries scheme for Scheduled Caste and Scheduled Tribes and 17.5 per cent share of funds will be utilized for works including roads and buildings. However, there will be no sectoral earmarking of resources at the Village Panchayat level except that 22.5 per cent of the annual allocation must be spent on items of works which directly benefit the Scheduled Castes and Scheduled Tribes.

Wages Under Jawahar Rozgar Yojana

Male or female workers under the Yojana may be paid partly in cash and partly in food grains. The rate of distribution of food grains will not exceed two kg. per man-day. The wages for a category of employment will be the same as notified for the relevant schedule of employment under the Minimum Wages Act. There should not be any attempt to avoid or evade, this mandatory obligation by denotifying an area or an employment from Minimum Wages Act. The State Government should identify those categories of employment under JRY for which a notification under Minimum Wages Act has not been issued. In all such cases, the wages should be notified as far as possible, under the Minimum Wages Act.

It has been observed that a duty had been cast on the employer to pay equal remuneration to men and women workers for same work or works of a similar mature as well as not to discriminate while recruiting men and women workers.[9] This provision of law may be brought to the notice of States Labour Department, which is responsible for issuing notification under the Minimum Wages Act, in case there is any deviation from the provisions of the Equal Renuneration Act for categories of employment for which Minimum Wages has not been notified under the Minimum Wages Act. Till such notifications are issued, payment may be made at the rates at which payment for similar categories of employment is being made by the State Government Departments such as Rural Engineering, Public Works Departments, Irrigation, Forest, Agriculture, etc. The executing agencies are responsible for payment of prescribed wages to workers engaged under the JRY Programme. Payment of wages should be made on a fixed day of the week which should preferably be the local market day. Payment of wages should not be delayed by more than a week except at the option of the workers and in the latter case for not more than fifteen days. In case the implementing agencies do not pay the wages for a category of employment at a rate notified for the relevant schedule of employment under the Minimum Wages Act, the Central Government will with hold grants to the State under the Jawahar Rozgar Yojana. The wage-material ratio under JRY will be 60:40. The wages paid to skilled labourers may be included under the wage component, subject to a limit of 10 per cent of the total wage cost. The expenditure on non-wage components comprising of the cost of materials, administrative and supervision expenses, cost of handling and transportation of materials and food grains etc., will be met from outside the Jawahar Rozgar Yojana funds. The main intention behind this type of wage system under Jawahar Rozgar Yojana Programme is to help the economically downtrodden people of the given society as they can improve, to a certain extent, their living conditions in the society. District Rural Development Authorities or Zilla Parishads prepare an Annual Action Plan in the preceding year before the beginning of each financial year. While preparing the Annual Action Plan, completion of the incomplete works are to be given priority over the taking of new works. It is also the responsibility of District Rural Development Authorities or Zilla Parishads are the sole authority to accord approval to the projects in respect of their share of funds. The plans for development of villages in the jurisdiction of different Village Panchayats that they must see that the work taken up under this JRY Programme would be completed within two financial years. The District Rural Development Authorities or Zilla Parishads are discussed thoroughly in the meetings of the Village Panchayat and the final decisions arrived at the meeting will determine the plan of works to be taken up during a particular year. While preparing the plan of works, care should be taken to safeguard the interests of the weaker sections in the village and paramount priority is given to the works benefiting the Scheduled Castes and Scheduled Tribes, women and others who are economically weaker in the village society. The Gram Sabha or village assembly must be appraised of the progress of implementation of the programme at least twice a year.

The works to be taken up under the Jawahar Rozgar Yojana Programme by the Village Panchayat are to be based on felt-needs of the people and importance is also given to the priorities indicated through the village assembly meetings. The paramount aim of the Jawahar Rozgar Yojana is to extend fiscal help to the majority of the economically weaker section of the village society. While there is no ceiling on the cost of works to be taken up under the JRY Programme, only such works will generally be taken up whose size and cost and nature are such that they may be implemented at the local level and do not involve a high level of technical inputs.

The Village Panchayats are competent to accord approval to the projects after they have been technically appraised and approved by the Panchayat Samithi or Intermediate Level Panchayat. At the village level, the development programmes are implemented through the Village Panchayats which will be responsible for planning and executing of the Yojana. The Village Panchayat is considered as the lowest elected body and includes Gram Panchayats, mandals or traditional institutions like Village Council and Village Development Boards having statutory character.

At the district level, the entire work relating to co-ordination, review, supervision and monitoring of the programme is vested in Zilla Parishads or District Rural Development Agencies. The total resources allocated to the state for implementation of the programme will be distributed to DRDAs or Zilla Parishads. They, in turn, have overall responsibility for supervision and monitoring the implementation of the programme and DRDAs and Zill Parishads are also made accountable to the State Government to ensure that the returns or reports in respect of the works taken up for execution in the district are furnished in time. In addition to this, the Village Panchayat also appoints a vigilance committee for the village under its jurisdiction to oversee, supervise, and monitor the implementation of the works under the Jawahar Rozgar Yojana Programme. This vigilance committee may consist of any persons living in the village and who, in the judgement of the Panchayat, will be of assistance to the Village Panchayat in this regard. Contractors are not permitted to be engaged for execuction of any of the works under the JRY Programme. No middleman or any such intermediate agency should be employed for executing works under this programme. However, there is every possibility that surrogate contractors in the names of villages youth coordinators, village organizers, etc. substituted the regular contractors under the wage employment programme. Hence, the Gram Panchayat must take abundant care that emergence of contractors in such devious wage is scrupulously avoided. The main intention of JRY Programme is to see that the full benefits of wages are to be paid to workers and the cost of the works does not go up on account of commission charges payable to such contractors, middlemen or intermediate agency.

For effective implementation of the programme, physical monitoring through field inspection is very important. Officers dealing with JRY at the state headquarters must visit the field regularly and must ascertain through field visits that the programme is being implemented satisfactorily and that execution of works is in accordance with the prescribed procedures and specifications. In the same way officers at the district and mandal levels also have to closely monitor all aspects of the programme through visits to work sites in area. A schedule of inspections, which prescribes the minimum number of field visits for each supervisory level functionary from the State Government to village level, should be drawn up and the concerned officials must strictly adhere to the same.

It is the responsibility of the State Government to prepare periodical reports through which it will also monitor the performance of the JRY activities in the districts. The State Government must also see that appropriate reports are to be collected by the District Rural Development Agencies or Zilla Parishads from the Village Panchayat for proper monitoring of the Jawahar Rozgar Yojana. These reports[10] would enable the authorities both at the centre and the state level to monitor the progress of the programme and to keep a close watch on the quality and trend of implementation and to take mid-course corrections. It is also suggested that in order to ensure social control of the Yojana, meetings of the Village Panchayat shall be held every month to consider the issues regarding the planning, execution, monitoring and supervision of the Jawahar Rozgar Yojana. These meetings may be open to any member of the village community, who shall be free to raise any issue regarding implementation of the Yojana Programme. The village assembly, to be held atleast twice a year, should also be kept informed about the progress of the implementation of Jawahar Rozgar Yojana and all other related issues.

It is also recommended that the officers handling JRY work at various levels are to be given orientation training at state level and Village Panchayat levels. While organizing training at the state level, organizations like Council for Advancement of 'Peoples' Action and Rural Technology, Central Building Research Institute, Central Road Research Institute, State Level Technical Institutions, Universities, State Institute of Rural Development and also competent non-governmental organisations should be involved, so that their expertise could be utilised for imparting training to the functionaries areas at different levels.

The fundamental objective of the training is to create awareness of the appropriate technology and various low cost techniques evolved with higher degree of labour intensity, and at the same time ensuring durability. Besides these, various operational details and implementation processes of the programme will be clarified during the training to functionaries associated with the implementation of the Jawahar Rozgar Yojana Programme.

It is also suggested that voluntary organizations may be involved in implementation of the programme at the district and Village Panchayat levels. The District Rural Development Agencies, Zilla Parishad and Village Panchayat may raise donations to expand the JRY Programme or to ensure the durability of the assets or to meet the non-wage expenditure. Contributions may also be accepted for similar purposes. Funds available from other sources like market committees, cooperatives, cane societies, charitable institutions and individuals also be dovetailed with the JRY funds for similar purposes.

Provision is also made in the JRY Programme that if there are any grievances in regard of the implementation of JRY by the implementing agencies, including proper payment of wages under the Jawahar Rozgar Yojana Programme, representations can be made to the higher authorities for redresses. In case of works executed by Panchayats, representations may be made to the District Collector. In the case of works executed by the District Rural Development Agencies or Zilla Parishads, the representation can be made to the District Collector and thereafter to the Divisional Commissioner or Secretary, Rural

Development Department of the State or representation can also be made to the Secretary in-charge of Rural Employment as the case may be. It will be the responsibility of these functionaries to enquire into the representation and refers the grievances in an appropriate manner.

Thus, the main objective of the JRY Programme is to alleviate of rural poverty. The prevalence of unemployment and under-employment in the rural areas is a contributing factor for high incidence of poverty at the rural level. The JRY Programme has given the main thrust to achieve the objective of poverty alleviation which in turn directed the JRY Programme towards creation of various works programme. Through its programmes, JRY is giving self-employment and wage employment to the poorer section of the community. It may be observed that the JRY Programme is primarily-oriented towards generating additional gainful employment for the unemployed and under-employed persons, both men and women, in the rural areas. Hence, the works under the Jawahar Rozgar Yojana Programme are undertaken for execution during any part of the year whenever the need for generating employment is felt.

In this chapter, an attempt is made to explain the different objectives of the Jawahar Rozgar Yojana Programme and an attempt is also made to explain in detail the different components of the Jawahar Rozgar Yojana Programme comprising food grains distribution under JRY, earmarking and utilization of resources of JRY, different works taken up under the programme, Indira Awaas Yojana, Million Wells Scheme, wage distribution under the programme, execution of works, criteria and procedure for allocation of funds, etc. Finally, an attempt is made by way of suggestions for effective monitoring and evaluation of the programme for its effective implementation keeping the overall development of the rural poor and the alleviation of rural poverty as well.

Notes

1. D.K. Desai, *Management in Rural Development*, Oxford and IBH Publishing Company, New Delhi, 1983, pp. 1-2.

2. P.R. Brahmananda, Narayan and Kalappa, (Eds.), *Dimensions of Rural Development in India*, Himalaya Publishing House, Delhi, p. 345.
3. C. Harichandran, *Panchayat Raj and Rural Development*, Concept Publishing Company, New Delhi, 1983, pp. 2-3.
4. B.C. Muthayya, Krishnama Naidu and Aneesuddin, *Behaviours Dimensions of Rural Leaders*, National Institute of Rural Development, Hyderabad, 1979.
5. Government of India, *JRY Manual* (Draft guidelines), Ministry of Agriculture, Department of Rural Development, New Delhi, April 1989.
6. Government of India, *JRY Manual for Villages* (As modified and effective from 1-4-1991), Department of Rural Development, New Delhi, June, 1991.
7. *Ibid.*
8. *Ibid.*
9. Refer Sections 4 and 5 of the Equal Remuneration Act, No. 25, 1976.
10. (i) A monthly progress report;

    (ii) A more detailed progress report;

    (iii) A detailed Annual Report.

    The first report is to be sent by 10th of every succeeding month.

    The quarterly report is to be sent by 25th of the month following the quarter; and the annual report is to be sent by 25th April of the succeeding year—According to the manual of JRY.

4

Target Group Participation

In the history of planned economic development process in India, the responsibility of planning and employment programme of such a magnitude as the JRY by the Gram Panchayats has been unlimited along with the power to take decisions on investment. It is indeed a milestone in the process of development through democratic decentralization. Huge amount is being spent every year in the implementation of JRY Programme. Such a massive wage employment programme requires expensive and systematic planning and implementation to fulfill the objective of generating additional gainful employment for the unemployed and underemployed in the rural areas, and to create durable community assets that strengthen the rural infrastructure and thereby lead to the growth of the rural economy.

There are about 19,540 Gram Panchayats in Andhra Pradesh, of which 18,372 are minor Panchayats, with an annual income of less than ₹ 4,000. There are a few thousand Panchayats which have practically no income. It is these small Panchayats which are expected to benefit mostly under the Jawahar Rozgar Yojana.[1] The modified version of guidelines issued by the Government of India suggest that the Yojana will be implemented as a centrally sponsored scheme on a cost sharing basis between the Centre and States in the ratio of 80:20.[2] The central assistance will be released to the States/Union Territories, which will further release to the districts, in accordance with the manner prescribed in the sanctioned letter of the Government of India, after adding their matching share. The JRY has the primary objective of generating additional gainful employment and the secondary objective of creating and strengthening rural assets and improving the overall quality of life.

The Zilla Parishads and Village Panchayats are the two main functionaries for the implementation of Yojana. The JRY has given a central place to the Panchayat Raj Institutions, viz. Zilla Parishads, Mandels and Village Panchayats. The Zilla Parishads prepare the annual action plan, equivalent to the value of 125 per cent of its share of funds in the preceding years, before the financial year. The Zilla Parishads is the sole authority to accord approval to the project. The total allocation which becomes available to the state for Jawahar Rozgar Yojana is distributed to the districts on the basis of prescribed norm, on the selection of projects. Each Zilla Parishad has a government body that looks after the JRY. It is headed by a District Development Officer, as its member secretary. Its members are the departmental heads from the development administration and officers of the concerned banks. Its non-officials include all the MPs of the district, nominated MLAs of the district, the representative of the SC/ST population and rural women. The invitees to these committees include Managing Directors of S.C. Corporation, all banks, Managers of main branches only, Collectors etc. This committee finalise the JRY plan for the district, supervises its function and monitors its performance. The district Development Officer of the Zilla Parishad is incharge of the planning of the programme. He is assisted by Executive Engineers (Panchayat Raj) and other district level officers.[3] He is also assisted by the members of Panchayat bodies and other non-officials.

In Ranga Reddy district, three Executive Engineers (Panchayat Raj) and ten Deputy Executive Engineers are functioning for three revenue divisions and 37 Mandals. The District is divided into 37 Revenue Mandals with 1055 villages and 583 Gram Panchayats. Added tho this, there the three Revenue Divisions, viz. Hyderabad East, Chevella and

Vikarabad. There are 37 Mandals, which comprise 982 habitated villages and 73 unhabitated villages.[4] At the Mandal level, the Mandal Panchayat is expected to play a major role. The president of the Mandal Panchayat and the Mandal Development Officer take major responsibility, and they are assisted by Deputy Executive Engineers and Assistant Executive Engineers and also by other elected members of the Mandal Panchayats. The plans for the development of villages in the jurisdiction of Village Panchayats/Mandals are discussed thoroughly at the meetings of the Panchayat, and the final decisions arrived at, are viewed as the plan works to be taken up during a particular year.

The Village Panchayats accord approval of the projects through Gram Panchayats meetings after they are technically approved at the level of Mandal Praja Parishad and District Development Authority. The Village Panchayats are supposed to frame estimate sanctions and measurement books, etc. Normally, the Assistant Executive Engineer checks measurement upto ₹ 20,000 while Deputy Executive Engineer has the authority upto the level of ₹ 20,000 and above, whereas the Executive Engineer has the power to check the measurements of ₹ 50,000 and above, per annum. The Mandal Development Officer clears the cheque after the fulfillment of the established guideliness.

The State Level Coordination Committee supervises and obtains appropriate returns and records from Zilla Parishads. A Central Committee set up by the Department of Rural Development in Krishi Bhavan at Delhi will oversee the progress and implementation of the programme. In case a Gram Panchayat has not selected body, the funds are passed on to the concerned Block, i.e. Mandal, which is the next higher elected local body so far as Andhra Pradesh is concerned. The Mandal Development Officer operates the funds, as in the case of other mandal works. The approvals are given by the Mandal Praja Parishads, in accordance with the guidelines.[5] According to JRY guidelines, a maximum of 5 per cent of the annual allocation, after earmarking 5 per cent to Indira Awaas Yojana are spent on administration/contingencies. The Government of

Andhra Pradesh issued a memo through which the state level committee decided to deduct 3 per cent of the allocation of source from the states matching share under JRY and to release the remaining 2 per cent of the allocation to the Gram Panchayats for making their own arrangement in regard to administrative and contingency expenditure relating to the implementation of JRY.[6]

The JRY guidelines envisaged that the central share as well as state share shall be exclusively deposited in separate savings bank account. The bank should be Nationalised, Scheduled/ Co-operative Bank. In the case of Ranga Reddy district of Andhra Pradesh, the amount was deposited in the banks until 1991-92, later it was credited to Government Treasury.[7] The accounts are audited by the Director of local fund audit, Government of Andhra Pradesh.[8] In accordance with the guidelines, the cheques shall be signed by the head of the Panchayat, Sarpanch, along with another person who can be a member of the Village Panchayat or Secretary of the Panchayat, i.e. the Executive Officer, in respect of notified Panchayats. Until 1990-91, the Sarpanch and Gram Panchayat member were drawing the amount by their signatures. In view of the fact that there was mis-appropriation by the Sarpanches, the said procedure was modified ever since 1991-92. The Mandal Development Officer and the Sarpanch were authorized to make joint signatures and draw the money. Owning to certain conflicts between Mandal Development Officer and the Sarpanch, the procedure was modified during the June 1992 through which a Group Executive Officer appointed for five villages was to append his signature, along with the Sarpanch for withdrawal of the money. The Group Executive Officer is also supposed to maintain the records such as muster foils, estimate copy, measurement book, cash book, pass book, the cheque book, etc.[9]

Performance of JRY at the State Level

As is known, the JRY has been under operation for the last nine years and significant progress was made under the JRY in Andhra Pradesh. A large number of durable community assets are said to have been created, which have contributed to the strengthening of rural infrastructure. The performance of JRY in the State of Andhra Pradesh is considered quite satisfactory. It is highly appreciated by the Central Government also. The performance of JRY in Andhra Pradesh during 1989-98 is shown in Table 4.1.

Table 4.1: Performance of JRY in Andhra Pradesh

Year	Annual outlay (₹ lakh)	Expenditure (₹ lakh)	Percentage to expenditure (₹ lakh)	Target of man-days	Actual Achievement (₹ lakh)	Percentage of achievement
1989-90	19,319.51	18,415.55	95.32	772.78	725.43	93.87
1990-91	19,166.20	19,317.09	100.79	920.35	805.08	87.47
1991-92	19,166.20	19,065.78	99.48	676.45	666.10	98.47
1992-93	21,480,22	19,339.39	90.03	659.75	667.10	101.11
1996-97	18,243,74	17,488.47	95.86	623.28	674.55	108.23
1997-98	19,850.81	19,373.94	97.60	642.25	686.76	106.93

Source: Annual Report, Department of Panchayat Raj and Rural Development, Government of Andhra Pradesh, Hyderabad, 1990, 1991, 1992, 1993, 1997, 1998

It may be observed that during 1989-90 the total resources allocated, including the matching share released by the State, and the Central Government, was around ₹ 19319.51 lakhs of which ₹ 18415.551 lakhs was utilized showing the achievement of 95.32 per cent. The target for employment generation was 772.78 lakh man-days, of which 725.434 lakh man-days was achieved showing 93.87 per cent net achievement. When we take the year 1990-91 into consideration, we find that the total outlay including the matching share released by both Centre and State Governments was ₹ 19166.20 lakhs. During this year, the total expenditure met towards the implementation of JRY in Andhra Pradesh was ₹ 19317.09 lakhs which is 100.79 per cent achievement. The target of employment generation during 1990-91 was 920.35 lakh man-days of which 805.08 lakh man-days were generated showing the net achievement to 87.48 per cent. Similarly, during 1991-92, the total annual outlay was ₹ 19166.20 lakhs which includes the matching share of the Central and the State Governments, ₹ 19065.78 lakhs was spent towards the employment generation which is 99.48 per cent achievement. During this year, the target for employment generation was fixed at 676.454 lakh man-days of which 666.10 lakh man-days were generated, which is 98.47 per cent achievement. It may be observed that during 1992 to 1993 the annual outlay towards JRY was ₹ 2148.22 lakhs, of which ₹ 19339.39 lakhs were spent towards employment generation showing a net achievement of 90.03 per cent in employment generation. The target fixed for employment generation was 659-75 man-days. However, the actual achievement in employment generation was 667.10 lakh man-days. The net achievement in employment generation exceeded the target showing 101.11 net achievement. It indicates an excess of 1.11 per cent over the total target fixed for the year. It may be observed that the performance of JRY in Andhra Pradesh relating to generation of employment during 1992-93 was phenomenal. The data pertaining to the year 1996-97 reveals that the annual outlay towards JRY was ₹ 18243.74 lakhs and ₹ 17488.47 lakhs were expended during this year for employment generation, showing 95.86 per cent net achievement. The target of employment generation was fixed at 623.28 lakh man-days, which the achievement had been 674.55 lakh man-days. In this year also the achievement shows a significant hike, because it had exceeded the target. Similarly, during the year 1997-98 the total annual outlay was ₹ 19850.81 lakhs of which ₹ 19373.94 lakhs were spent showing an achievement of 97.60 per cent. The target for employment generation was 642.25 lakh man-days. However, a total of 686.76 lakh man-days was generated, which indicates an excess of 6.93 per cent over the entirely of the target fixed for the year. In the case also the achievement had been spectacular, because it had exceeded the target. It may be observed that during the years 1992-93 to 1997-98 the actual employment generation exceeded the target fixed. Similarly, the data pertaining to the performance of JRY in Ranga Reddy district is presented in Table 4.2.

It may be observed that during 1995 to 1996 the total availability of funds for JRY in Ranga Reddy district was ₹ 1432.37 lakhs which includes ₹ 4167 lakhs carry over from previous year, and ₹ 1390.7 lakhs, the actual release of grant during the year 1995-96. From this total amount, the District Development Authorities have spent an amount of ₹ 1392.94

lakhs for the employment generation in the district showing an achievement of 97.245. The target for employment generation was 23.85 lakh physical man-days. However, a total of 23.878 lakh man-days was generated indicating 0.11 per cent of excess over the target during the year.

Table 4.2: Performance of JRY in Ranga Reddy District

Category	1995-96	1996-97	1997-98
1. Carry over from previous year	41.67	39.43	109.92
Release during the year	1390.70	902.28	1034.09
Total availability (₹ lakh)	1432.37	923.66	1144.01
Annual Outlay			
2. Expenditure (₹ lakh)	1392.94	831.79	1097.03
3. Per cent of expenditure	97.24	90.05	95.89
4. Target of physical man-days	23.85	15.80	17.50
5. Actual achievement of man-days	23.88	15.83	24.64
6. Percentage of achievement	100.11	100.18	140.77

Source: Annual Reports, District Development Officer, Zilla Praja Parishad, Ranga Reddy District, 1996, 1997, and 1998

When we take the year 1996-97 into consideration we find that the total availability of funds was ₹ 923.66 lakhs which includes ₹ 39.43 lakhs, carry over from previous year, and ₹ 902.28 lakhs release by the state during the year. From this total availability of ₹ 923.66 lakhs, ₹ 831.79 lakhs were utilized for the employment generation showing an achievement of 90.05 per cent. The target for employment generation during the year 1996-97 was 15.80 lakh physical man-days of which 15.83 lakh man-days were generated showing 100.18 per cent achievement. Insofar as the 1997-98 data is concerned, the total availability of resources were to the order of ₹ 1144.01 lakhs which includes ₹ 109.92 lakhs, carry over from previous year, and ₹ 1034.09 lakhs, state's release during the year 1997-98. The resources utilized accounted to ₹ 1097.03 lakhs which is 95.98 per cent achievement. The target of employment generation was fixed at 17.50 lakh physical man-days. However, a total of 24.035 lakh man-days was generated, which indicates an excess of 40.77 per cent over the entirety of the target fixed for the year. In other words, the performance relating to generation of physical man-days during 1997-98 is phenomenal and it may be observed that the achievement, in employment generation, is spectacular, because it had exceeded the target fixed.

It may be observed that Jawahar Rozgar Yojana is the largest single employment programme. The primary objective of JRY is to create additional gainful employment for the unemployed and underemployed persons both men and women in the rural areas. The Yojana is also intended to create assets in favour of rural poor, particularly Scheduled Castes and Scheduled Tribes for their direct and continuing benefits. Hence, the people below the poverty line will be treated as the target groups under Jawahar Rozgar Yojana. However, preference is given to Scheduled Castes, Scheduled Tribes and freed bonded labourers for employment under the Yojana while 30 per cent of the employment opportunities under the Yojana will be reserved for women. The Yojana is also motivated with the creation of sustained employment by strengthening rural economic infrastructure and to create community and social asset as well. At this juncture, an effort is made to present the data pertaining to the category-wise distribution of employment generation under Jawahar Rozgar Yojana in Ranga Reddy district (Table 4.3).

Table 4.3: Category-wise Distribution of Employment Generation Under JRY in Ranga Reddy District

Sl.No.	Category	1995-96	1996-97	1997-98
1.	Scheduled Castes	3.581	2.138	4.503
2.	Scheduled Tribe	1.432	.0855	1.491
3.	Others	18.865	11.266	18.641
4.	Total	23.878	14.259	24.635
5.	Percentage	Above 100	Above 100	Above100
6.	Women	7.880	4.705	8.094

Source: Annual Reports, District Development Officer, Zilla Praja Parishad, Ranga Reddy District, 1996, 1997 and 1998

The data presented in Table 4.3 shows that during 1995-96, the total employment generation under JRY in Ranga Reddy district was 23.878 lakh man-days, showing an achievement more than 100 per cent, of which 3.581 lakh man-days were in favour of Scheduled Castes showing an achievement of 14.99 per cent. The employment generation among the Scheduled Tribes was 1,432 lakh man-days showing an achievement of 5.99 per cent, whereas the employment generation among other rural poor is 18.865 lakh man-days showing an achievement of 79 per cent. Women are also given an employment amount to 7.880 lakh man-days. Similarly, during 1996-97, the total employment generation under JRY in Ranga Reddy district was 14.259 lakh physical man-days contributing above 100 per cent net achievement. During this year, the employment generation among Scheduled Castes was 2.138 lakh man-days showing 14.99 per cent achievement, among Scheduled Tribes the figure was 8.855 lakh man-days showing 5.996 achievement. The employment generation among others was 11.266 lakh man-days contributing to 79.009 per cent achievement. When we take the year 1997-98 into consideration we find that the total employment generation during this year is 24.635 lakh man-days, which is treated as above 100 per cent achievement. During this the employment generation among Schedule Castes is 4.503 mandays contributing to 18.2 per cent net achievement. Among the Scheduled Tribe target group, the employment generation is 1.491 lakh man-days days contributing to 6.052 per cent net achievement. However, the employment generation among others is 10.641 lakh physical mandays showing 43.194 per cent achievement. During this year, the employment generation from among the target group of women is 8.094 lakh man-days. It is significant to note that during 1995-96, 1996-97, and 1997-98 the employment generation under JRY in Ranga Reddy district is shown above 100 per cent net achievement. Similarly, the data pertaining to physical performance (in lakh man-days) and employment generation under Jawahar Rozgar Yojana in Ranga Reddy district is collected for the three consecutive years 1995-96, 1996-97 and 1997-98 and the date is presented in Table 4.4. The data pertaining to the year 1997-98 shows the physical performance and employment generation until the release of the second installment grant.

The analysis of data in Table 4.4 shows that the total physical performance and employment generation during the year was 641.620 lakh physical man-days, of which 177.087 (27.59 per cent) was shown under scheduled target group, 105.807 (16.49 per cent) lakh man-days was shown under the category of Scheduled Tribes target group and others have got 358.666 (53.90 per cent) lakh man-days of physical performance and employment generation under JRY, during 1996-97, the total physical performance and employment generation under JRY was 299.80 lakh man-days. The employment generation among the Scheduled Castes target group was 134.91 lakh man-days constituting 45 per cent achievement. The physical performance and employment generation among Scheduled Tribes target group was 44.97 lakh man-days constituting to 14.989 per cent net achievement and the employment generation among the other was recorded at 119.92 lakh man-days showing 40 per cent achievement. Similarly, during the year 1997-98, the availability of records is up to the release of Second installments grants, the total physical performance and employment generation under JRY 99.03 lakh man-days. The total physical performance 24.548 per cent achievement. The Employment generation among Scheduled Tribes is 13.07 lakh man-days contributing to 13.198 per cent achievement and the physical performance and employment generation under Jawahar Rozgar Yojana for others is 61.65 lakh man-days constituting 62.253 per cent achievement.

Table 4.4: Physical Performance (in lakh man-days) and Employment Generation Under JRY in Ranga Reddy District

Sl.No.	Category	1995-96	1996-97	1997-98
1.	Scheduled Castes	177.087	134.910	24.310
2.	Scheduled Tribes	105.867	44.970	13.090
3.	Others	358.666	119.920	61.650
4.	Total	641.620	299.800	99.050
5.	Landless	404.220	269.820	64.430
6.	Women	218.150	104.930	35.840

Source: Annual Reports, District Development Officer, Zilla Praja Parishad, Ranga Reddy District, 1996, 1997 and 1998

It is also significant to note that during 1995-96, landless target groups were also benefited though the JRY by way of employment generation to the tune of 404.220 lakh man-days. During the year 1996-97, employment generation among landless was 269.82 lakh man-days and among women it was 104.93 lakh man-days. During 1997-98, the employment generated for landless was 64.43 lakh man-days. The physical performance and generation of employment for women was 35.84 lakh man-days. The analysis of data shows that the performance of Jawahar Rozgar Yojana in Ranga Reddy district is quite satisfactory and at the same time the District Development Authorities are attaining above 100 per cent achievement.

The Jawahar Rozgar Yojana is expected to enable the house holds to cross poverty line through its developmental schemes. In a way, availing of the benefits extended by the public policy, constitutes positive participation of the people in the development programmes. Active participation of the people would help not only the target groups to avail themselves of the benefits that percolate from above, but also to articulate their demands and get what they need. In the process, people would develop the capacity to devise development schemes based on their life experiences, understanding of local needs, requirements and resources. In this regard, it may be observed that rural poor should collectively share to implement the schemes with mutual understanding and put their best in this effort. It is from this perspective that participation should be conceived as a key component in ensuring effectiveness of public policy.

The success of the public policy depends upon peoples' participation because increasing participation would rest on increasing awareness. This awareness in them would be a result of exchange of ideas and information among the people. This type of increasing consciousness among the people can always be helpful in inculcating scientific attitudes, proper orientation and acceptance of the programme. Public participation through their own organization would also ensure greater accountability of the system to the people. It may be observed that increasing participation means more of communication from the people to the government. The distortions in information flow can be avoided through well organized people's associations which root out the middlemen or contractors who, for their own reasons, act as channels of communication and provide the missing link between the government and the people. In their place, more responsible intermediaries would emerge on whom people will have control thus enforcing greater accountability. It is also said that organized effort through conscious participation can facilitate effective monitoring of the programme and continuous evaluation.

Participation of Target Groups

It is almost universally accepted that no economic development can take place without the participation of the people. Through participation, people would gain increasing control over their own destinies and their dependence on government would get reduced. The JRY Programmes are target-oriented anti-poverty programmes. Their focus is basically on the disadvantaged groups in the rural society who have not been able to benefit much from several other developmental programmes. In this chapter, an attempt is also made to examine the phenomenon of the target groups participation on the basis of empirical data. For this purpose, an attempt is made to examine the dependence of the people on governmental support. The respondents were asked whether the developmental schemes should be taken up only by the government. The data is presented in Table 4.5.

Table 4.5: Respondents Opinion about the Need for Government Adoption of Development Schemes

Sl. No.	Opinion of the Respondents	No. of Respondents	Per Cent
1.	Govt. alone can take up	265	88.33
2.	Govt. need not take up	27	9.00
3.	Do not know	8	2.67
	Total	300	100.00

The data presented in Table 4.5 shows that 88.3 per cent respondents thought that the government alone should take up these schemes. Out of 300 respondents 27 (9.0 per cent) noted that the government need not take up all these programme and 8 (2.7 per cent) respondents could not answer this question. To the question as to why government should take up these programme, the respondents justified their answer saying that it is the responsibility of the government to help the rural poor to cross the poverty line. They have also said that none else is competent and powerful as the government to command the resources to undertake these schemes, and in addition to this, they also feel that the people are so poor that they cannot take up anything without the help of the government. It is also observed that government alone can advance loans which do not involve exorbitant interest as is the case with the money lenders who are highly exploitative.

One important trend can be traced out from the above responses that a majority of the people could not think of any alternative to government and feel that the government is resourceful and impartial and they also think that it is the responsibility of the government to help the rural poor. Moreover, people at large are also viewed as an alternative to take up the schemes on their own, but this was also dropped on the grounds that people are illiterate, poor, inefficient, quarrelsome and cannot discriminate between what is desirable and what is not. In fact, poverty as a reason figured very prominently for the inability of the people to take up any developmental schemes on their own. As a result, the government emerged as the only organisation to take up the developmental responsibilities. The negligible number of respondents who said that government should not take up these programmes felt that government was indifferent and inefficient. They also expressed their opinion that schemes taken up by the people on their own can be implemented efficiently. At this level, the respondents were asked about the schemes under JRY that government had been undertaking for the benefit of Scheduled Castes, Scheduled Tribes, women, landless, and freed bonded labourers at the rural level. The data is presented in Table 4.6.

Table 4.6: Statement Showing the Awareness of Jawahar Rozgar Yojana Programme

Sl.No.	Awareness of JRY	No. of Respondents	Per cent
1	2	3	4
1	Heard	278	92.67
2	Not heard	22	7.33
	Total	300	100.00

The data presented in Table 4.6 reveals that out of 300 respondents, 278 (92.7 per cent) had heard about the JRY programmes and only 22 (7.3 per cent) of the respondents stated that they have not heard about the JRY Programme. This reveals the fact that majority of rural poor in Ranga Reddy district are aware of JRY intended has the rural upliftment. The respondents who had heard of the JRY Programmes were asked about the objectivities of the JRY. An overwhelming number of them responded that JRY is mainly intended to alleviate rural poverty and they also revealed that it is the largest single employment programme generating gainful employment for the unemployed and under-employed persons in the rural areas. At this juncture, the respondents were asked to list the different works under JRY, the data is presented in Table 4.7.

Table 4.7: Statement Showing the Opinion of the Respondents about the Different programmes under JRY

Sl. No.	Awreness of Different Programmes	No. of Respondents	Per Cent
1.	Construction of houses	133	44.33
2.	Development of allotted land	32	10.67
3.	Social forestry work	46	15.33
4.	Minor irrigation wells	18	6.00
5.	Drinking water wells	18	6.00
6.	Nurseries	29	9.67
7.	Poultry units	24	8.00
	Total	300	100.00

The data presented in Table 4.7 shows that all the respondents stated that they are aware of some of the programmes under JRY 133 (44.3 per cent) of the respondents stated that they are aware of construction of houses under

JRY, 32 (10.7 per cent) respondents have noted that they know about the programme of development of allotted land in the case of allottees of ceiling surplus land, Bhoodan land, government land whether they belong to Schedule Caste or Schedule Tribe category or not, 46 (15.3 per cent) respondents have noted that they know about social forestry works such as fuel wood and fodder plantations and agri-horticulture group, 29 (9.7 per cent) respondents have noted that they know about the nursery programme under JRY, 24 (8 per cent) respondents knew about the poultry units programme and the remaining 36 (12 per cent) respondents had mentioned the minor irrigation wells and drinking water wells under JRY. However, a majority (44.3 per cent) of respondents know that house construction work can be taken up under JRY for the benefit of the identified individuals below the poverty line.

The respondents were asked about the difficulties faced in getting the scheme and the data is presented in Table 4.8.

Table 4.8: Opinion of Respondents about the Difficulties in Getting the JRY

Sl. No.	Facing Difficulties	No. of Respondents	Per Cent
1.	Faced difficulties	210	70.00
2.	Not faced difficulties	72	24.00
3.	No response	18	6.00
	Total	300	100.00

The data presented in Table 4.8 reveals that out of 300 respondents 210 (70 per cent) of the respondents have noted that they did not face any difficulties in getting and implementing to schemes under JRY, 72 (24 per cent) difficulties in getting and implementing the schemes under JRY. It may be observed that the impact of JRY depends not only on the giving of schemes but also on the way that were implemented and subsequently maintained and therefore, it is considered important to discuss the problems of getting and implementing the scheme JRY. When asked to spell the type of difficulties they faced in this regard, the respondents claimed that there are pilferage at various points and they have to part with their savings in the hope of getting benefits of the scheme. Some of the complaints concerned the delay in getting the scheme sanctioned. It was stated that they had to go several times to government offices for getting the schemes.

Another type of difficulty was related to technical problems such as location of the spot for a new well, delay in getting the report from the geologist and initial clearance for the well. A specific question was asked about the length of delay in getting the schemes. It ranged between one month to more than eight months. The data is presented in Table 4.9.

Table 4.9: Time Taken to Get the Scheme Sanctioned under JRY

Sl.No.	Time Taken	No. of Respondents	Per cent
1.	One month	17	22.67
2.	Three months	18	24.00
3.	Four months	17	22.67
4.	Five months	18	24.00
5.	Six months	4	5.33
6.	Eight months	1	1.33
	Total	75	100.00

The data presented in Table 4.9 shows that 75 respondents made mention about the length of delay in getting the schemes in terms of months. Seventeen respondents had mentioned that it took one month for them to get the scheme sanctioned, 18 (24 per cent) of the respondents mentioned three months, 17 (22.7 per cent) respondents mentioned four months, another 18 (24 per cent) respondents quoted five months, 4 respondents mentioned six months, whereas only one respondent had mentioned eight months delay in getting the scheme sanctioned to him. However, it is significant to note that a majority of 70 (93.4 per cent) of the respondents have noted that it took between one and five months for them to get the scheme sanctioned under JRY. As for the nature of the difficulties faced in the implementation of the programmes, on the economic side, there were complaints that the amounts sanctioned under the scheme were found to be insufficient because of cost increase in the infrastructure, which they could not afford to pay in addition to the scheme amount, and, on the technical side, several of them found technical assistance too inadequate. In terms of economy, the family poverty and other domestic demands like marriages, ill-health of family members, social and religious rites, etc. accounts for the diversion of funds meant for the scheme.

A question was administered to the beneficiaries as to whether they had been benefitted by the JRY or not. The opinion of the respondents is presented in the form of data in Table 4.10.

Table 4.10: Opinion of the Respondents on the Benefit from the JRY Scheme

Sl.No.	Opinion of the Respondents	No. of Respondents	Per Cent
1.	Benefited	282	94.00
2.	Not benefited	12	4.00
3.	Do not know	6	2.00
	Total	300	100.00

The analysis of the data presented in Table 4.10 shows that out of 300 responents, 282 (94 per cent) of the respondents reported that they are benefited by the schemes under JRY whereas 12 (4 per cent) of the respondents have reported that they have not received much benefit under the scheme of JRY because they felt that to derive benefits from the schemes the economic status is more important than the social status. According to them, the majority from the higher income group and larger land holding class which included Scheduled Castes and Scheduled Tribes and others reported as having been benefited. The beneficiaries were asked to state that the impact of the schemes had been in terms of increase in income and additional employment which were the main objectives sought to be achieved through the Jawahar Rozgar Yojana. The opinion of the respondents is presented in Table 4.11.

Table 4.11: Opinion of the Respondents about the Additional Employment Generated by the JRY

Sl. No.	Opinion of the Respondents	No. of Respondents	Per Cent
1.	Generated	285	95.00
2.	Not generated	9	3.00
3.	Do not know	6	2.00
	Total	300	100.00

The data presented in Table 4.11 shows that out of 300 respondents, 285 (95 per cent) had opined that the schemes under JRY had created employment for the unemployed and underemployed rural poor and only a negligible number of respondents (3 per cent) have noted that the schemes under JRY have not created or generated additional employment. This shows that the fundamental objective of JRY is being fulfilled in Ranga Reddy district by way of generating additional employment to unemployed and underemployed persons both men and women, in the rural area and the JRY had also led to the creation of sustained employment by strengthening the rural economic structure.

It may be observed that the participation of people in developmental programmes is partly determined by linkages between the elite groups and the people in the village. Here an attempt is made to find out the attitude of the people in maintaining contact with the elite in the village. The data is presented in Table 4.12.

Table 4.12: Contacts with the Elite in the Village

Sl. No.	Contact with the elite	No. of respondents	Per cent
1.	Meet	286	95.33
2.	Do not meet	14	4.67
	Total	300	100.00

The data presented in Table 4.12 shows that out of 300 respondents, 286 (95.3 per cent) of the respondents stated that they regularly meet or in contact with the elite groups in their villages. Only 14 (4.7 per cent) of the respondents stated that they do not meet the elite group of their villages very regularly. However, the linkages between the elite groups and the people in villages would provide cordial atmosphere in implementing the various schemes under JRY in rural areas. Their attitude towards different members of the elite groups in village would provide an insight into the elite-mass relations and the role the elite can play in mobilising support of the people for developmental programmes. In this connection, a question was administered on the respondents as to whom they met usually in their villages. The responses show that the village officer, viz. Patwari or Karnam, the Sarpanch, upa-Sarpanch, the police patel are the persons whom the village meet frequently. The Samithi President or Ex-Samithi President also figured in the above category. The other members of the elite group are the leaders of castes, landlords, teachers, businessmen. A few respondents also mentioned friends and relatives. In this connection, the respondents were asked to express their opinion on the general behavioural style of the village elders. The data is presented in Table 4.13.

The data in Table 4.13 reveals that out of 300 respondents, 167 (55.7 per cent) of the respondents stated that the elite are unhelpful in their attitude towards the poor whereas 109 (36.3 per cent) of the respondents held the opinion that the elites of their villages take a favourable and helpful attitude towards them and 24 (8 per cent) of the respondents declined to answer the question.

Table 4.13: Statement Showing the Opinion of the Respondents about the Attitude of the Village Elite towards the Programme

Sl.No.	Attitude of the Respondents	No. of Respondents	Per cent
1.	Helpful	109	36.33
2.	Not helpful	167	55.67
3.	Do not know	24	8.00
	Total	300	100.00

The respondents were asked the reasons why the elite adopted an unhelpful attitude towards them. A large number of respondents suspected that elite groups work against the development of the poor and they also opined that elite are the losers if the poor prosper. They also expressed the opinion that the elite have become corrupt, selfish and therefore do not take a helpful attitude towards the poor. The main intention behind these responses has been that the elite are bent upon oppressing the poor. This, according to the respondents, explains the hostility of the elite towards them. This also partly accounts for the increasing dependence of the poor on the government.

The respondents who have expressed the view that elite groups are helpful have said that elders in the villages helped them in securing government loans and the elders provide them moral support in the case of any crisis. They also expressed the opinion that the elders pursue the schemes and get them sanctioned from government and they look after the welfare of the village. This pattern indicates that people perceive the village elite only as a channel through which the governmetal schemes flow to the village. As a result, the elite lost their autonomous entity and are being replaced by the government.

The participate dimension is also dependent upon the co-operation that exists. In view of this, a question is administered on the respondents about who should decide the schemes to be taken up for the benefit of the rural poor under JRY. The data is presented in Table 4.14.

The data presented in Table 4.14 shows that out of 300 respondents, 132 (44 per cent) of the respondents stated that the poor people should decide about the developmental schemes implemented under JRY whereas 94 (31.3 per cent) of the respondents are of the opinion that all the villagers should collectively decide together about the schemes to be taken up for benefit of the people under JRY. 32 (10.7 per cent) respondents have expressed the opinion that elite in the village should decide about the schemes to be implemented in their villages under Jawahar Rozgar Yojana. It is significant that 42 (14 per cent) respondents felt that the schemes taken up for the benefit of the rural poor under Jawahar Rozgar Yojana should be left to the choice of the government itself.

Table 4.14: Statement Showing the Opinion of the Respondents about Those who Decide the Scheme Under JRY

Sl.No.	Attitude of the Respondents	No. of Respondents	Per Cent
1.	All the villagers should decide	94	31.33
2.	The elite in the village should decide	32	10.67
3.	The poor people in the village should decide	132	44.00
4.	It has to be left to the choice of the government itself	42	14.00
	Total	300	100.00

Another dimension of participation deals with peoples' understanding of the causes of and solutions to poverty. For this purpose, an attempt has been made to analyse their perceptions of poverty on the one hand and the solutions they had in their mind for these problems on the other. It was thought that this would provide an insight into the attitudinal pattern which is crucial to an understanding of the participative phenomenon. The respondents were asked to give the causes for existence of poverty in villages. The opinion of the respondents is presented in Table 4.15.

The data presented in Table 4.15 shows that out of 300 respondents, 148 (49.3 per cent) respondents felt that since land is central to economic life, poverty is the result of landlessness. 86 (28.7 per cent) respondents felt that bad habits of the poor people such as estravagence, unnecessary expenditure on social and religious items, drinking habits are the fundamental causes for existence of poverty in villages. 44 (14.7 per cent) respondents traced poverty to the failure of monsoon frequently whereas 22 (7.3 per cent) respondents felt that poverty exists because of the gap between the rich and the poor and exploitation of the latter by the former.

Table 4.15: Statement Showing the Opinion of the Respondents about the Causes for Existence of Poverty in Villages

Sl.No.	Attitude of the Respondents on Causes of Poverty	No. of Respondents	Per Cent
1.	Landlessness	148	49.33
2.	Failure of monsoon	44	14.67
3.	Exploitation of the rich	22	7.33
4.	Population explosion and bad habits	86	28.67
	Total	300	100.00

In this connection, the respondents were asked about the measures for eradication of poverty in villages. The opinion of the respondents is presented in Table 4.16.

Table 4.16: Opinion of the Respondents on the Measures for Eradication of Poverty

Sl.No.	Opinion of Respondents	No. of Respondents	Per Cent
1.	Increasing assistance in the form of government programmes	146	48.67
2.	Increase in the agricultural wages	78	26.00
3.	Provide additional employment	64	21.33
4.	Do not know	12	4.00
	Total	300	100.00

The data in Table 4.16 shows that 146 (48.7 per cent) respondents favoured eradication of poverty through governmental programmes. In fact, most of the solutions they suggested revolved around Jawahar Rozgar Yojana schemes and objectives. 78 (26 per cent) respondents pleaded for an increase in agricultural wages, whereas 64 (21.3 per cent) respondents asked for the provision of additional employment for unemployed and underemployed to improve the economic conditions of the rural poor. The responses indicate that an overwhelmingly large number sought development programmes such as generation of additional gainful employment, creation of community assets and improving the overall quality of life in the rural areas through governmental programmes and support. Thus, they think that their poverty can be eradicated through government support. Hence, a question is administered on the respondents to find out their attitude in regard to their support extended to Jawahar Rozgar Yojana being implemented by the government. The data is presented in Table 4.17.

Table 4.17: Opinion of the Respondents about Their Support to JRY

Sl. No.	Opinion of Respondents	No. of Respondents	Per Cent
1.	Strongly support	284	94.67
2.	Oppose	4	1.33
3.	Do not know	12	4.00
	Total	300	100.00

The data presented in Table 4.17 shows that 284 (94.7 per cent) respondents have overwhelmingly supported the Jawahar Rozgar Yojana because it is mainly intended for the upliftment of the rural poor whereas only 4 (1.3 per cent) respondents did not support the JRY without giving proper reasons and 12 (4 per cent) respondents maintained silence over this question. Basing on this, the respondents were asked to compare the existing conditions with the conditions prevailing in the days of their parents. The data is presented in Table 4.18.

The data presented in Table 4.18 shows that 262 (87.3 per cent) respondents reported that there is an improvement in the conditions when compared with the olden day 12 (4 per cent)

respondents have noted that there is no change in the situation and 8 (2.7 per cent) respondents have stated that there is a deterioration in the conditions of the rural people compared to the days of their parents. And 18 (6 per cent) respondents have not replied to this question. Those who thought there is an improvement in conditions stated that today the government is more helpful than in the past. A few of them also felt that because of the development programmes there has been more work and therefore more income. Quite a few of them observed that people had more food and modern facilities such as electricity, etc. and there were also a few who said that practices like bonded labour were now disapproved. Those who felt that they did not find any change in the conditions said that there has not been any addition either to their property or income. The frequent failure of the monsoon stagnated the living conditions. Quite a large number of them held that increase in their wages had been mentioned by increase in the prices and they also felt that they were solely dependent on their physical labour right from ancestral times and found no difference in the conditions. Those who said that they perceived deterioration have stated that inflation and increasing prices account for stagnation and deterioration. They also drew attention to the degeneration in the ethical values of the society. They also stressed failure of the monsoon, increase in the cost of inputs, expenditure on social functions such as marriages, education, etc. These causes they thought had resulted in the deterioration in the living conditions of the rural poor.

Table 4.18: Opinion of the Respondents on the Comparison of the Existing Conditions with the Past

Sl.No.	Opinion of Respondents	No. of Respondents	Per Cent
1.	There is improvement in the conditions	262	87.33
2.	No change	12	4.00
3.	There is deterioration in the condition	8	2.67
4.	Do not know	18	6.00
	Total	300	100.00

In this chapter, an attempt has been made to evaluate the implementation of Jawahar Rozgar Yojana in Ranga Reddy district and an effort is also made to analyse the target group participation in JRY. It may be observed that the performance of JRY in Ranga Reddy district is quite satisfactory. In other words, the performance of JRY in Ranga Reddy district relating to generation of physical man-days during 1995-96, 1996-97 and 1997-98 is phenomental and it may be observed that the achievement, in employment generation, is very spectacular, because it had exceeded the target fixed. It may be observed that public participation is crucial for development. In anti-poverty schemes like Jawahar Rozgar Yojana, the participation of target groups can ensure effectiveness of the policy. In one aspect, the target groups take advantage of the benefits extended to them and in another aspect they not only avail themselves of the benefit but articulate their needs and demands. In this regard, it may be observed that 88.3 per cent (Table 4.18) respondents thought that government alone is competent enough to important such schemes because none else is powerful and competent as the government to command the resources. The awareness of 278 (92.7 per cent) respondents about the JRY about that Reddy district is aware of JRY which is intended for rural upliftment. It is significant to note that overwhelming majority (70 per cent) of the respondents have stated that they had not faced any major difficulty in getting and implementing the schemes under JRY is within easy reach of rural poor. 282 (94 per cent) respondents have noted that they are benefited by the schemes under JRY by way of additional employment generation to unemployed and under employed at the rural level.

The rural people in Ranga Reddy district are maintaining linkage with the elite group of their villages and this reveals their participation in the development schemes under JRY. The participative dimension is also dependent upon the cooperation that exists among the people. The analysis of the data shows that 44 per cent (Table 4.14) respondents stated that the poor people should decide about the developmental schemes under JRY.

The rural respondents in Ranga Reddy district are of the opinion that poverty is the result of landlessness. In addition to this, they also perceive that failure of monsoon frequently, population explosion and bad habits, etc. are some of the other important causes for existence poverty in villages and hence 146 (48.7 per cent) respondents asked for increased assistance in the form of governmental programmes. They also pleaded for an increase in agricultural wages and for the rural unemployed and underemployed to be provided additional employment regularly for their economic and social upliftment. Hence, 284 (94.7 per cent) respondents have strongly supported the JRY because it is intended for the upliftment of the poor and majority of the rural poor in Ranga Reddy district had accepted that there is an improvement in their conditions when compared with the older days. Thus, it may be observed that JRY implementation in Ranga Reddy district is quite satisfactory.

References

1. S.P. Ranga, "Give Panchayats Operational Freedom under JRY", *Kurukshetra*, Vol. XXXVIII, No. 4, January 1990.
2. Government of India, *JRY—Manual for Villages (As modified and effective from 1-4-1991)*. Department of Rural Development, New Delhi, 1991.
3. Government of Andhra Pradesh, *Guidelines for JRY*, Department of Panchayat Raj and Rural Development, Hyderabad.
4. Government of Andhra Pradesh, *Ranga Reddy District Hand Book*, Department of Statistics, Hyderabad, 1995.
5. G.O. No. 17040/NREP.III/89, dated 20.6.1989, Hyderabad.
6. Memo No. 35090/NREP, III/89, Hyderabad.
7. Memo No. 33026/JRY-3/92-93, dt. 23.5.1992, Hyderabad.
8. Memo No. 69380/NREP/III/89-3, dt. 31.10.1989, Hyderabad.
9. Memo No. 69693/e.VI/91, Panchayat Raj and Rural Development, Hyderabad, dt. 25.11.1995.

5

Role of Elites in JRY—Performance of JRY in Ranga Reddy District

The emerging social, economic, political trends in a society accentuate increasing dependence of people on the governmental machinery. The elite in a developing society have a crucial role to play. Representatives of the people are considered to be the substitute for public participation in a democratic context. In a democratic society, it is observed that public representatives occupying key positions have to maintain rapport with the people and have to act as effective links between the government and the people. The elite in the rural society are treated as the instruments for articulation of rural needs and demands of the rural people on the one hand and have to moblise people's support for developmental schemes on the other. In short, the elite groups and public representatives have to enjoy public confidence.

Generally, the rural people depend on their village elders in securing government loans. People will have confidence in their representatives saying that they pursue the developmental schemes and get them sanctioned from the government. This pattern indicates that people perceive the village elite as an important channel through which the governmental schemes flow to their rural areas. In this chapter, an attempt is made to study the opinion of the rural elite on various aspects of

Jawahar Rozgar Yojana. The researcher interviewed altogether 84 persons belonging to elites groups in the Ranga Reddy district whose socio-economic profile and their perceptions as well as views are given below.

Table 5.1: Statement Showing the Elite Sample

Sl. No.	Nature of Sample Elite	No. of Respondents	Per cent
1.	Mandal Presidents	4	4.76
2.	Sarpanches	20	23.81
3.	Upa-Sarpanches	20	23.81
4.	Gram Panchayat Ward Members	40	47.62
	Total	84	100.00

A sample of four mandals was selected, one each from three revenue divisions. Similarly, from each mandal five villages were chosen which totally accounts for 20 villages. Therefore, 20 village Sarpanches and 20 Upa-Sarpanches were chosen. Besides, two ward members in each village stretching over to a total of 40 ward members were interviewed among the four mandals. Thus, the sample comes to 84, which represents the rural elite in Ranga Reddy district. It may be observed that the 84 elites are chosen from mandal presidents who constitute 4.3 per cent, Sarpanches and Upa-Sarpanches constitute 23.8 per cent each and the ward members constitute 47.6 per cent.

Table 5.2: Statement Showing the Sex Composition of the Elite

Sl.No.	Sex	No. of Respondents	Per Cent	Sarpanches Only	
				No. of Respondents	Per cent
1.	Male	76	90.5	16	80.0
2.	Female	8	9.5	4	20.0
	Total	84	100.00	20	100.0

The data presented in Table 5.2 shows that out of a sample elite of 84 members, 76 (90.5) are male members and 8 (9.5) are female elite. Male Sarpanches number is 16 while the female Sarpanches are 4 in strength, accounting for 80 per cent and 20 per cent respectively. It may be observed that the female elite are very few in the entire district and therefore, their representation within the sample corresponds to the

Universe. It may be noted that the implementation of policy measures of providing 30 per cent reservation to women in rural and urban local bodies will substantially increase the representation to women in the rural and urban local bodies.

Table 5.3: Caste Composition of the Sample

Sl.No.	Caste	No. of Respondents	Per Cent	Sarpanches Only	
				No. of Respondents	Per cent
1.	Forward Castes	22	26.19	12	60.00
2.	Backward Castes	43	51.19	5	25.00
3.	Scheduled Castes	17	20.24	2	10.00
4.	Scheduled Tribes	2	2.38	1	5.00
	Total	84	100.00	20	100.00

The data presented in Table 5.3 indicates the composition of elite within the sample. It is evident that Forward Caste elite are 26.2 per cent of the total sample, while those coming from the Backward Caste are 43 in number and 51.2 per cent of the total sample, the Scheduled Caste are 20.2 per cent while Scheduled Tribes are 2.4 per cent. It may be pointed out that the representation to Backward Caste is more or less uniform with that of their absolute proportion within the Universe. However, in the case of Scheduled Castes, there seems to be some disproportion when compared to their composition within the society. So is the case with that of the Scheduled Tribes. In the case of the Sarpanches, it may be pointed out that 12 Sarpanches constituting 60 per cent belong to Forward Caste, five Sarpanches constituting 25 per cent belong to Backward Caste, two Sarpanches from Scheduled Caste constituting 10 per cent and one Sarpanch constituting 5 per cent are found among the Sarpanches. It may be noted that the representation to Forward Caste is quite phenomenal from among the elected Sarpanches, while their representation to Backward Caste, Scheduled Caste and Scheduled Tribes is very poor. Such a lopsided representation indicates that the dominance of Forward Caste in view of wealth, resources and other characteristic features is quite strong. The representation to Backward Castes, Scheduled Castes and Scheduled Tribes from among the Sarpanches is substantially poor. Their enhanced representation is possible with suitable protective discrimination. Although in the case of other elites like Upa-Sarpanches, ward members, there is considerable representation to such castes, yet in matters of Gram Sarpanches the pattern of representation is low.

Table 5.4 illustrates the rural-urban habitation of the elite within the sample. It may be observed that in a total of 84 elite within the sample, 70 elite constituting 83.3 per cent actually reside in rural parts, while 14 elite constituting 16.7 per cent inhabit urban areas. From among them, 12 Sarpanches constituting 60 per cent, inhabit rural areas while eight Sarpanches constituting 40 per cent inhabit urban parts.

Table 5.4: Statement Showing the Habitation of Sample Elite

Sl.No.	Habitation	No. of Respondents	Per Cent	Sarpanches Only	
				No. of Respondents	Per cent
1.	Rural	70	83.33	12	60.00
2.	Urban	14	16.67	8	40.00
	Total	84	100.00	20	100.00

By and large, majority of the rural elite reside in rural areas only. Just 16.7 per cent of the elite, though elected from the Gram Panchayat, continue to maintain their developing concern in urban parts only. Such a type of elite, in view of their popularity and other characteristic features, despite not residing in rural parts, continue to get elected to the rural local bodies. Insofar as the elected Sarpanches are concerned, 60 per cent continue to live with the rural population, while 40 per cent, though getting elected to Gram Panchayats, remain outside such rural areas. Inabsentia leadership is not conducive to the effective functioning of the rural local bodies which ultimately contribute to the successful implementation of the JRY Scheme. The elite elected from certain rural areas are supposed to dwell among such rural people and evince interest in rural matters.

For effective implementation of JRY in ensuing rural development, it is necessary to provide orientation to the officers handling JRY work at various levels. Training arrangements will have to be made at State/DRDA/

Panchayats/Mandal levels. Regular training workshops or programmes should be organized for this purpose. Therefore, to know the opinion of the elite at the rural level, a question pertaining to training received by the elite is administered and the data is presented in Table 5.5.

Table 5.5: Whether Training Received in Jawahar Rozgar Yojana

Sl.No.	Catagory	No. of Respondents	Per Cent	Sarpanches Only	
				No. of Respondents	Per cent
1.	Yes	18	21.43	3	15.00
2.	No	66	78.57	17	85.00
	Total	84	100.00	20	100.00

The data in Table 5.5 shows that out of 84 elite within the sample 66, elite within the sample constituting 78.6 per cent had revealed that proper training arrangements have not been made at the State or Village Panchayats level for their specific purpose and hence they expressed the view that they could not get proper training in this context, whereas 18 elite, constituting 21.4 per cent, have received some form of training. Further, among the elite who had some sort of training only three Sarpanches, constituting 15 per cent. It is significant to mention that those who had undergone such training had invariably indicated that it was just a nominal affair stretching over half-a-day meeting held at mandal headquarters, giving them a brief outline of the schemes of JRY. It may be mentioned that for the orientation to the rural elite with JRY Scheme during the last few years, such meetings lasting for half-a-day duration were held occasionally. It is evident that training had been treated as a casual affair by the district authorities who do not seen to have taken seriously the work of imparting orientation to the rural elite in general and the Sarpanches and the Upa-Sarpanches in particular. As the scheme is quite important and much money of the Central and State Governments is being spent over it, it is necessary that the rural elite properly guided and trained.

In view of the immense significance of the Jawahar Rozgar Yojana, the Union and the State Governments have particularly taken care to provide the Jawahar Rozgar Yojana

Manual to all the Village Panchayats for guidance and observance of necessary norms. It is expected of the Village Panchayat Sarpanches particularly to follow the said manual and confirm to rules and regulations in the implementation of the scheme. In this context, a question is administered to the elite to know whether Jawahar Rozgar Yojana Manual is available in the Panchayat office and the opinion of the elite is presented in Table 5.6.

Table 5.6: Statement Showing the Availability of Jawahar Rozgar Yojana Manual

Sl.No.	Catagory	No. of Respondents	Per Cent	Sarpanches Only	
				No. of Respondents	Per cent
1.	Yes	36	42.86	9	45.00
2.	No	48	57.14	11	55.00
	Total	84	100.00	20	100.00

It is evident from Table 5.6 that 36 respondents of the elite have confirmed the availability of the said manual in the Panchayat office, which accounts for 42 per cent of the total. Among these 36 respondents constituting 42 per cent have affirmed the said view. On the other hand, 48 respondents from among 84 elite, constituting 58 per cent, have denied the availability of such manual in the office. Among them 11, elite are the Sarpanches of the Village Panchayats, who account for 58 per cent. By and large, the responses amply denote that they seem to have not taken care in obtaining a copy of the said manual for frequent reference work. In the absence of the manual, there is every possibility that the Village Panchayat staff, including the Sarpanches, rely mostly on their memory in regard to guidelines. However, relying on one's memory is improper. It is appropriate that the Gram Panchayat office invariably obtain a copy of the said manual, not only for their guidance, but also for the general information of the public. The State Government should take necessary steps for the provision of manuals to all the Gram Panchayat office.

It may be observed that the successful and effective implementation of developmental schemes depends upon sufficient personnel requirement for its implementation. Lack of sufficient number of personnel also creates hurdles in the successful implementation of the development at schemes. In this context, a question is administered to the elite about the persons assisting Panchayat in implementing the JRY and the data is presented in Table 5.7.

Table 5.7: Persons Assisting Panchayat

Sl.No.	Name of the Officer	No. of Respondents	Per cent
1.	Group Executive Officers/Village Development Officer	69	82.14
2.	Sarpanch-clerk/Karobari/Panchayat Secretary	15	17.86
	Total	84	100.00

To a question as to the personnel assisting the Village Panchayat in matters of Jawahar Rozgar Yojana, it may be observed that the Group Executive Officer is identified by 69 respondents, constituting 82.15, while 15 elite have identified a clerk or Karobari or Panchayat Sarpanch constituting 17.9 per cent. Normally, the Group Executive Officer/Village Development. Officer services as many as five villages. The State Government had appointed him, in the month of April 1992 (Govt. Memo. No. 69693/E.VI/91, dt. November 25, 1991), exclusively for Jawahar Rozgar Yojana work only. Prior to the appointment of Village Development Officer, the work related to Jawahar Rozgar Yojana was carried on by the Sarpanches and they maintained all the accounts relating to Jawahar Rozgar Yojana. Thus, Village Development Officer or Group Executive Officer held additional charge of the Jawahar Rozgar Yojana work which is indeed quite burdensome for carrying on the necessary work. There is thus an immense need for the recruitment of necessary personnel for effective implementation of the Jawahar Rozgar Yojana scheme as well as the proper maintenance of records pertaining to the Gram Panchayat.

As and when the Rozgar Yojana funds are released through the District and Mandals to the respective Village Panchayats, it is a normal practice for the Sarpanches to convene a meeting of the Gram Panchayat members to discuss the nature of works to be undertaken and their consent is obtained for undertaking the said activities, keeping in view the money that is provided and budget formulated. Such a kind of formulation is known as Annual Action Plan. In this context, a question has been administered to the elite asking whether annual action plan had been prepared by a Village Panchayat for the works taken up under Jawahar Rozgar Yojana in the past. The response pattern is presented in Table 5.8.

Table 5.8: Formulation of Action Plan

Sl.No.	Catagory	No. of Respondents	Per Cent	Sarpanches Only	
				No. of Respondents	Per cent
1.	Yes	52	61.90	14	70.00
2.	No	32	38.10	6	30.00
	Total	84	100.00	20	100.00

The data presented in Table 5.8 shows that out of 84 respondents, 52 (61.9 per cent) respondents had revealed that annual action plan is formulated wherein the nature of work to be undertaken is discussed in the meeting of the Gram Panchayat members and consent of the members is taken for the implementation of the work under JRY, keeping in view the money that is provided by Central and State Governments. Among them, 14 (70 per cent) Sarpanches also confirmed that the meeting of the Panchayat members is convened by the Sarpanches of their Village Panchayat. However, 32 (38.1 per cent) elite have affirmed the above opinion, and among them, there are six Sarpanches constituting 30 per cent. These elite within the sample are of the view that proper action plan is not formulated and depending upon the situation and circumstances, they used to spend the budget amount towards the constructive activities of their village. It is suggested that annual action plan is essential for the proper utilization and effective implementation of the JRY schemes and hence the State Government should see wherever and whenever funds are released, that it should be spent according to the annual action plan to minimize the wastage and to undertake proper development work keeping in view its future and present utilisation.

In every Village Panchayat, there is a Gram Sabha or Village Assembly constituted by all the people of that village. The meeting of the Village Assembly has to be held at least twice a year wherein any member of that village community is force to raise any issue regarding implementation of the Jawahar Rozgar Yojana. In the meetings of the Gram Sabha, discussion will take place on the progress of the implementation of Jawahar Rozgar Yojana and all other related issues. Village Assembly may be considered as the basic unit of the village which has control over the utilization of funds in regard to JRY. Village Assembly has the power to decide the items of works to be taken up under Jawahar Rozgar Yojana at its meetings. In this context, a question is administered to the elite within the sample whether the Gram Sabha meetings are taking place in the village and the response pattern in presented in Table 5.9.

Table 5.9: Gram Sabha Meeting to Discuss Action Plan

Sl.No.	Category	No. of Respondents	Per Cent
1.	Yes	23	27.38
2.	No	61	72.62
	Total	84	100.00

There is a general criticism against the meeting of the Gram Sabha on the grounds that the meetings are not held as per the schedule. Hence, the village community people always criticise their elected representatives for not holding the meeting as and when required to discuss about the implementation of JRY in their village and they are deprived of their opportunities in expressing their opinion before the Village Panchayat. The data presented in Table 5.9 also confirm the same, wherein 61 (72.6 per cent) respondents are of the opinion that the meetings of Gram Sabha are not held regularly to discuss the action plan for the JRY programmes, whereas 23 (27.4 per cent) respondents stated that the Gram Sabha meetings are held to discuss the plans for development of their village. The Village Panchayat is appraised of the progress of implementation of the JRY Programme. It may be suggested that wherever the Gram Sabha meetings are not taking place atleast twice in a year, the elected Panchayat must take into account the Gram Sabha and discuss the action plan. So that works which are useful to the entire village community may be undertaken under Jawahar Rozgar Yojana. The works to be taken up under the Jawahar Rozgar Yojana Programme by the Village Panchayat should preferably be selected based on the full needs of the people and the priorities must be indicated through the Village Assembly meetings.

Works taken up under the Jawahar Rozgar Yojana Programme would be of durable standards and specifications. It has been mentioned in the Yojana manual that full advantage should be taken of the rural technology available under the Rural Development Department. The Village Panchayat shall be competent to accord approval to the projects after they have been technically appraised and approved by the district authorities. In this aspect, it may be observed that the projects approved under the Jawahar Rozgar Yojana are at times delayed for want of technical appraisal. Hence, there is every possibility for the projects being kept pending at the mandal level while seeking technical approval. This type of delay in implementing the project hinders the development of the rural society. In this context, a question is administered to the elite to know their opinion about the delay caused in keeping the projects pending for want of technical approval. The response pattern is presented in Table 5.10.

Table 5.10: Delay in Approving the Projects at the Mandal Level Seeking Technical Approval

Sl.No.	Pending Duration	No. of Respondents	Per Cent
1.	One month	67	79.76
2.	Two months	12	14.29
3.	More than two months	5	5.95
	Total	84	100.00

It may be observed that the delay in approving the projects for want of technical approval may make the beneficiaries loose their faith in the timely assistance extended by the government. The data in Table 5.10 shows that out of 84 respondents, 67 (79.8 per cent) respondents stated that their projects were kept pending for one month, 12 (14.3 per cent) respondents mentioned that the delay took two months and five (5.9 per cent) respondents stated that their projects were delayed for more than two months for want of technical approval. It is suggested that, as far as possible, pending may be avoided to help the rural poor in getting implementation of the Jawahar Rozgar Yojana projects. The timely assistance may help them a lot to overcome the difficulties in their lives.

The primary objective of Jawahar Rozgar Yojana is to create community and social assets. The creation of assets is intended in favour of the rural poor, particularly the Scheduled Castes and Scheduled Tribes, for their direct and continuing benefit to improve the overall quality of life in the rural areas. Under Jawahar Rozgar Yojana, beneficiary-oriented individual programmes for economically weaker sections including Scheduled Castes and Scheduled Tribes can be taken up, viz. construction of houses, development of allotted lands, social forestry works, minor irrigation wells and group wells. In this context, a question is administered to the elite whether the assets created under the Yojana are meeting the needs of the community. The data is furnished in Table 5.11.

Table 5.11: Creation of Assets Meeting the Needs of the Community

Sl.No.	Category	No. of Respondents	Per Cent
1.	Yes-Meeting the needs of the community	67	79.76
2.	No-It is not meeting of the community	12	14.29
3.	Partly meeting the needs of the community	5	5.95
	Total	84	100.00

The data presented in Table 5.11 shows that out of 84 respondents, 52 (69.5 per cent) respondents have stated that the assets created under the Jawahar Rozgar Yojana are meeting the community needs because the developmental works undertaken under the Yojana are approved by the Village Panchayat taking the ratification from the Village Assembly. However, 22 (26.2 per cent) respondents noted that the works undertaken or assets created under the Jawahar Rozgar Yojana are, at times, not completed in time and hence could not meet the community needs. Some have expressed the view that, at times, the division of opinion among the village poor also reflects on the work taken up under the Jawahar Rozgar Yojana which are not in a position to satisfy the collective needs of the community and thereby results in dissatisfaction. So much so, 10 (11.9 per cent) respondents are of the opinion that the assets are not meeting the community needs. However, to satisfy each and every one in the society is highly impossible because of the existence of selfish nature and hence it is suggested that the Gram Panchayat, before approving the works to be implemented under the Jawahar Rozgar Yojana, must take into account the common and social needs of the village which would result in the upliftment of the entire village and rural poor including Scheduled Castes and Scheduled Tribes as well.

Table 5.12: Statement Showing the Opinion of the Respondents about the Quality of Work and Assets Created under JRY

Sl.No.	Opinion of Respondents	No. of Respondents	Per Cent
1.	Good	32	44.44
2.	Satisfactory	36	50.00
3.	Poor	12	16.67
4.	Do not know	4	5.56
	Total	84	100.00

To a dependent question asking about the quality of work and assets created for community needs under Jawahar Rozgar Yojana Schemes, Table 5.12 shows that 32 (38.1 per cent) respondents reported that the quality of works or assets created under JRY are good and in accordance with the technical approval of the expertise, whereas 36 (42.8 per cent) respondents noted that they are satisfactory and 12 (14.3 per cent) respondents noted that the assets created under JRY are poor in quality because of insufficient funds given under the Jawahar Rozgar Yojana. However, it may be observed that the assets created under JRY in Ranga Reddy district are satisfactory in regard to quality, but at the same time, owing to the fluctuation in construction costs, the beneficiaries are violating their demand that the funds are also to be liked along with the price hike so that two permanent assets are created and the JRY will have the quality to be utilised by the future generation also.

The assets created under the Yojana should be taken over by the concerned regular departments of the State Government or Panchayat Raj institutions and should also be maintained by those departments of Panchayat Raj institutions. Maintenance of assets created under the employment programme for which maintenance funds are not ordinarily available shall be done by the village panchayat or mandal with the funds made available to them for that purpose under the Yojana. Whenever plantation has been taken up under the farm forestry and agri-horticulture under the Jawahar Rozgar Yojana on community land and for community benefits, the loss of maintenance of such plantation up to the period of year from the year of plantation, may be met from JRY funds. In this context, a question is asked to know the opinion of the respondents in regard to the maintenance of the assets created under JRY and the data is presented in Table 5.13.

Table 5.13: Proper Maintenance of the Assets

Sl.No.	Maintenance of the Assets	No. of Respondents	Per cent
1.	Maintained by Panchayat	52	61.9
2.	Maintained by Mandal	12	14.3
3.	Maintained by Concerned Dept.	8	9.5
4.	Maintained by Communities	12	14.3
	Total	84	100.0

The data presented in Table 5.13 shows that out of 84 respondents, 52 (61.9 per cent) of the respondents noted that the assets created under JRY are maintained by the Village Panchayat, 12 (14.3 per cent) respondents noted that they are maintained by the village communities. In Ranga Reddy district, the fact that the assets created under the JRY are looked after by the mandal or Panchayat Raj institutions make us undersand that in order to keep the assets for their continuous existence, the concerned departments or Panchayat Raj institutions are taking great care. Though the available funds are limited, the maintenance of assets created under JRY is given sufficient care. The success of the programme is also dependent upon the proper maintenance of the assets created under JRY.

The muster rolls for all works under JRY should have entries showing Scheduled Castes/Scheduled Tribes/landless/free bonded labour/women workers. The officials responsible for the preparation of muster rolls should be responsible for these entries also. The concerned officials while signing the muster rolls should also record on the muster rolls at the time of weekly payments, a certificate indicating the employment generation for the Scheduled Castes, the Scheduled Tribes and for others, as also the total employment generated. It is stated that the employment generation figures should be completed from the certificates of the muster rolls. Supervisory level officers should check the employment-generation reports and the certificates on the muster rolls during their inspection. It is alleged that there is every possibility for them. In this context, the opinions of the respondents are gathered about the authenticity of muster rolls. The latest date is presented in Table 5.14.

Table 5.14: Statement Showing the Opinion of the Respondents about the Authenticity of Muster Roll

Sl.No.	Opinion of the Respondents	No. of Respondents	Per Cent
1.	Authentic	61	72.6
2.	Cooked up	14	16.7
3.	Do not know	9	10.7
	Total	84	100.0

The data provided in Table 5.14 shows that 61 (72.6 per cent) respondents stated that the muster rolls maintained by officials responsible are authentic in nature because they are subjected to inspection by the higher officials meant for the same. Any variation or misutilisation of muster rolls may lead to the violation of responsibility and hence subjected to punishments. However, 14 (16.7 per cent) respondents noted that the officials responsible for the preparation of muster rolls may cook up the figures and may try to misutilise the funds meant for the developmental works. However, it may be suggested that the government should impose stringent punishments on the officials who tend to misutilise the muster rolls for their individual benefits. Otherwise it may lead to improper implementation of JRY Programmes meant for rural development.

According to the manual of the Jawahar Rozgar Yojana, it is stated that arrangements must be made for providing facilities like drinking water, rest sheds for the workers and crèches for the children coming with working mothers. Expenditure involved for providing these facilities should be met out of the non-wage component under the Yojana. In this context, a question is administered whether arrangements are made for providing facilities like rest sheds and crèches for the children coming with working mother and the response pattern of the elite is shown in Table 5.15.

Table 5.15: Provision of Facilities at the Work Sites

Sl.No.	Category	No. of Respondents	Per Cent
1.	Yes	14	16.7
2.	No	70	83.3
	Total	84	100.0

The data presented in Table 5.15 shows that out of 84 respondents, 70 (83,3 per cent) respondents noted that such arrangements of facilities are not provided properly either for workers or working mothers for the reason that the funds received are sufficient only for the works and for the wage and hence they are not in a position to provide facilities like work sheds for the workers or crèches for children coming with the working mother. Hence, should be taken to the spare sufficient funds within the released grants for the works to be undertaken under the JRY instead of providing the expenditure for such facilities out of non-wage component under the Yojana. It may be observed that for the success of the JRY programmes, the involvement of voluntary organisations is very essential. Voluntary organizations should be involved in implementation of the programme at the district and village Panchayat level whenever possible. In this context, a question is administered to the elite within the sample to express their opinion about the involvement of voluntary organizations. The data is presented in Table 5.16.

Table 5.16: Involvement of Voluntary Organisation

Sl.No.	Category	No. of Respondents	Per Cent
1.	Yes	52	61.9
2.	No	32	38.1
	Total	84	100.0

The data presented in Table 5.16 shows that out of 84 sample elites, 52 (61.9 per cent) elite within the sample noted that suitable local voluntary agencies with proven good track record whenever available are associated with the works like construction of houses. At times the supervision, guidance and the maintaining of construction are entrusted to these voluntary organisations. The services of voluntary organisations are also used to popularize the use of sanitary latrine and also in the construction of smokeless chullahs. However, 32 (38.1 per cent) respondents stated that the participation of voluntary agencies in the works undertaken under JRY in rural areas is not satisfactory. Youth organizations at the rural level are distracted from their voluntary services by certain political attitudes. Some of the respondents also felt that the services extended by voluntary organisations may not suit the needs of the rural poor. These obstacles are hindering the voluntary organisations from taking active part in the JRY works. However, it may be suggested that the Panchayat Raj institutions may involve the voluntary organisations to extend their help in the construction activities of JRY which would certainly improve the quality of the works and may reduce the construction cost met by the rural poor.

Million Wells Scheme was launched as a sub-scheme of National Rural Employment Programme and Rural Landless Employment Guarantee Programme during the year 1988-89 and since continued during 1989-90 as a sub-scheme of Jawahar Rozgar Yojana. Million Wells Scheme was launched with the objective of providing open irrigation wells, free of cost, to poor, small and marginal farmers belonging to Scheduled Castes, Scheduled Tribes and freed bonded labourers. Million Wells Scheme allocation is primarily intended for open wells, only and tube wells and bore wells are not to be taken up under this provision. Where wells are not feasible owing to geological factors, the amounts allotted under this scheme may be utilized for other schemes of minor irrigation like irrigation tanks, water harvesting structures and also for the development of lands belonging to small and marginal farmers. In the present day situation, the open wells are not in a position to complete with the tube well or bore well systems and hence the open wells are becoming less useful. In this regard, a question is administered to the elite within the sample to know about their opinion about the open wells and the data is presented in Table 5.17.

Table 5.17: Preference to be Given to Tube Wells or Bore wells than to the Open Wells

Sl.No.	Category	No. of Respondents	Per cent
1.	Yes	73	86.9
2.	No	11	13.1
	Total	84	100.0

The data presented in Table 5.17 shows that a majority of 73 (86.9 per cent) of the elites within the sample are in favour of tube wells or bore wells. They put forward the reason that there will be less wastage of water either by way of evaporation or from the point of view of utilization. They are of the opinion that the funds available under this scheme meant for open wells may at times be provided to the bore wells systems depending upon the situation. In this respect, it may be suggested that the government may think over it and may provide a provision for transfer to bore wells depending upon the given situation based on the opinion of the majority of beneficiaries. It may be observed that the financial assistance is extended to Village Panchayats by the State Government in three instalments depending on the completion of works under the Jawahar Rozgar Yojana. There is a general demand from the beneficiaries that financial assistance may be given in one instalment. In this regard the opinion of the elite within the sample is collected and the data is presented in Table 5.18.

The data presented in Table 5.18 shows that out of 84 elites within the sample, 64 (76.2 per cent) respondents are of the opinion that the financial assistance may be extended to Village Panchayat in one instalment so that the beneficiaries may be in a position to complete the work in time without waiting for the release of instalment. They also felt that the release of funds in instalments may not at times meet the variation in the cost of construction due to rise in the cost of materials, and, at times, the delay in releasing the instalments may take them loose their faith on the timely assistance of the Government. However, 13 (15.5 per cent) respondents also felt that three-instalment release of assistance is a lengthy process and felt that it may be paid in two instalments which may be considered as neither lengthy nor burdensome to government. At times, the non-availability of funds at a stretch may make the government to provide the assistance in instalments. Providing the assistance in two instalments may reduce the burden of both the beneficiaries and the government.

Table 5.18: Statement Showing the Opinion of the Sample Elite on the Release of Assistance

Sl.No.	Release of Funds	No. of Respondents	Per Cent
1.	In one instalment	64	76.2
2.	In two instalments	13	15.5
3.	No answer	7	8.3
	Total	84	100.0

To a dependent question whether the funds released under JRY are sufficiently adequate for the works undertaken, Table 5.19 shows that 76 (90.5 per cent) elite within the sample gave a negative answer saying that the funds are hardly sufficient for the works which are implemented under JRY Programme. It may be observed that the government had fixed the wages and material ratio to the extent of 60:40. Under JRY, the beneficiaries and the elite within the sample are of the opinion that the cost of the materials required for construction purposes are increasing year by year and the funds released under the JRY are not sufficient to meet the increasing cost of the materials. It is suggested that depending on the cost increase, the assistance may also be increased instantly to meet the needs of the rural poor for their social and economic development. The plans pertaining to the works undertaken under JRY are generally prepared and estimated by the mandal office. They will be approved by the higher authorities and Villages Panchayats as well. In this context, a question is administered to the elites and the data is presented in Table 5.20.

Table 5.19: Opinion about the Adequacy of Funds Released under JRY

Sl.No.	Category	No. of Respondents	Per Cent
1.	Yes, adequate	8	9.5
2.	No, not adequate	76	90.5
	Total	84	100.0

Table 5.20: Preparation of Plans and Estimates by Mandal

Sl.No.	Category	No. of Respondents	Per Cent
1.	Properly	76	90.5
2.	Not Properly	8	9.5
	Total	84	100.0

The data presented in Table 5.20 shows that 76 (90.5 per cent) respondents stated that the preparation of plans and estimates are properly done by the mandal office whereas 8 (9.5 per cent) respondents affirmed the above opinion saying that there are some laxities in the preparation and estimation of works by the mandal office. Based on this, another question is administered to the elite within the sample asking whether the technical guidance is provided properly by the distance or state administration. The data is presented in Table 5.21.

Table 5.21: Whether Technical Assistance or Guidance Provided Properly

Sl.No.	Category	No. of Respondents	Per Cent
1.	Yes	22	26.2
2.	No	62	73.8
	Total	84	100.0

The data in Table 5.21 shows that out of 84 sample elite, 62 (73.8 per cent) respondents are of the opinion that sufficient technical guidance is not extended to them by the higher authorities and, at times, this will result in higher expenditure and lower quality of work. However, 22 (26.2 per cent) respondents are of the opinion that they are provided with sufficient technical guidance for the proper implementation of the works under JRY. It may be suggested that works taken up under the programme should be of a amenable nature and should meet appropriate technical standards and specification. The specifications for different type of works at the DRDA or Zilla Parishad level should be the same as approved by the State Government for similar type of works. Encouragement should be given to the use of low cost technology and local materials and efforts should be made to utilize local materials and low cost technology developed by various institutions keeping all these facts in view it may be suggested that proper technical guidance may be provided to the beneficiaries and to the implementing authorities as well.

Distribution of food grains as part of wages under rural employment programme is based on the principle of protecting the real wage of the workers besides improving the nutritional standards of the families of the rural poor. Food grains should invariably be given as part of wages under Jawahar Rozgar Yojana in view of its sustained benefits to the rural poor at the rate of 2 kg per man-day. Generally, the food grains for the Yojana will be released to the states in instalments along with the release of other Jawahar Rozgar Yojana resources. In this context, a question is administered about the providing food grains as part of wages. The data is presented in Table 5.22.

Table 5.22: Providing Food Grains as Part of Wages under JRY

Sl.No.	Category	No. of Respondents	Per cent
1	2	3	4
1.	Yes	22	26.2
2.	No	62	73.8
	Total	84	100.0

The data presented in Table 5.22 shows that 62 (73.8 per cent) respondents stated that food grains as a part of wage under Jawahar Rozgar Yojana are not paid to the workers because, at times, the food grains are available in the open market at prices cheaper than those prescribed under the public distribution system, and if the workers are provided food grains towards their wages, those workers engaged under Jawahar Rozgar Yojana will be at a disadvantage. However, 22 (26.2 per cent) respondents noted that food grains are distributed as part of wages under rural employment programme under Jawahar Rozgar Yojana. In order to avoid the disadvantageous position of the workers, which may occur during some months in a year, it may be suggested that the distribution of food grains under Jawahar Rozgar Yojana may be made optional depending upon the prices in the open market.

To a question pertaining to the misappropriation of funds, majority of the elites within the sample are of the view that there is a great scope for such misappropriation of funds either by the sanctioning and implementing authorities on one side, or by the beneficiaries on the other. In order to reduce the misappropriation of funds under Jawahar Rozgar Yojana, it may be suggested that the Village Panchayat should appoint a vigilance committee for each village under its jurisdiction to oversee, supervise and monitor and implementation of the works under the programme. This committee may consist of any persons living in the village and who, in the judgement of the Panchayat, will be of assistance to it in this regard and must include at least one representative of the Scheduled Castes or Scheduled Tribes. It may be observed that surrogate contractors by the name of village youth co-ordinators, villages organizers or similar other names are substituted for the regular contractors under the wage employment programmes. Care should be taken to avoid such contractors who indulge in devious methods to restrict the misappropriation of funds under Jawahar Rozgar Yojana. Both physical and financial audit of the works implemented by the Village Panchayats are to be made compulsory.

To a question pertaining to the displaying of the details of works on wall-posters or notice board at the Village Panchayat or Mandals, a majority of the elites stated that it has not been done. However, it is suggested that such type of displaying on the wall-posters or notice boards will give wide publicity to the Jawahar Rozgar Yojana, and at the same time, there is every possibility that a majority of the rural people will get an idea of the schemes and will develop a faith in the constructive activities of the government and may utilise the programme for their overall development.

In this chapter, an effort is made to study the elite perception on Jawahar Yojana in Ranga Reddy district. Generally, the rural people depend on their village elders and with the confidence reposed in them, they pursue the developmental schemes and get them sanctioned from the government. It may be observed that there is a dominance of Forward Castes in the elite group of Ranga Reddy district. Though there is considerable representation to Backward Castes, Scheduled Castes and Scheduled Tribes in the case of elite groups like Upa-Sarpanches, ward members, yet in the case of group Sarpanches, the pattern of representation is dominated by the Forward Castes because of wealth, resources and other characteristic features. About 40 per cent of the elected Gram Panchayat remain outside their rural areas and it appears that leadership in absentia is still in vogue in Ranga Reddy district. It is suggested that the elite getting elected from rural areas should reside in rural parts only and must get themselves involved in rural development. It may be said that the effective implementation depends upon the training received by the officers handling JRY works at various levels and hence it is necessary that the rural elite in Ranga Reddy district be properly trained in different aspects pertaining to Jawahar Rozgar Yojana and every Gram Panchayat office in Ranga Reddy district should invariably obtain a copy of the JRY Manual for general information both for the officials and public.

Lack of sufficient personnel is a hurdle in the way of successful implementation of JRY. In Ranga Reddy district, there is an immense need for the recruitment of necessary personnel for the effective implementation of JRY schemes and for the proper maintenance of records. Preparation of action plan is essential for any type of developmental schemes. In Ranga Reddy district, though a proper action plan is prepared for the implementation of the Yojana schemes, Gram Sabha meetings are not held according to the Schedule. Therefore, it is suggested that the meetings of the Gram Sabha should be held at least twice in a year to discuss the action plan pertaining to the JRY. Again, delay in implementing the projects may not meet the stated ends, hence, it may be suggested that timely help may be extended to the beneficiaries for reaping the fruitful benefits under the Jawahar Rozgar Yojana schemes.

The implementation of projects under Jawahar Rozgar Yojana in Ranga Reddy district is helping in the creation of social assets depending upon the community needs and the quality of works are also to the satisfaction of the technical expertise and are properly maintained by Panchayat, Mandal and other concerned departments as well as by the communities in Ranga Reddy district. In regard to the pattern of release of grants under Jawahar Rozgar Yojana, a majority of beneficiaries and elites have expressed their opinion that the releasing of grants at a time is good for the successful implementation of JRY schemes. At the same time, they have also stated that funds under the Jawahar Rozgar Yojana may be enhanced keeping in view the hike in the cost of materials used in the developmental schemes under JRY. The data pertaining to the preparation of plans and estimation reveals that they are properly done by the concerned officials and, at the same time, it may be suggested that proper technical guidance may be provided to the beneficiaries and to the implementing authorities as well. It may be observed that the distribution of food grains towards the wages under JRY may, at times, create certain disadvantages to the workers engaged under JRY. Therefore, the distribution of food grains under JRY may, be made optional depending upon the prices in the open market. On the whole, the implementation of JRY in Ranga Reddy district is quite satisfactory as per the norms prescribed by the government.

6

Conclusions

The field of public policy has assumed considerable importance in response to the increasing complexity of the society. It is not only concerned with the description and explanation of the causes and consequences of government activity, but also with developing scientific knowledge about the forces shaping public policy.

Public policy may be considered as an important mechanism for moving a social system from the past to the future and it has assumed considerable importance in modern times. The modern state uses public policy as an important sources of legitimization and justification for the existence. In fact, the welfare state has had its origins in the transformation of the state from its totally coercive character to the assumption of a developmental role. The poverty and deep rooted inequalities in society call for increasing intervention of the state to accelerate the process of social change.

A comprehensive study of public policy begins with a systematic enquiry into the various forces that shape the policy which are known as the inputs into the policy. The analysis of the policy content includes the decisions and actions of the government in pursuance of the policy. The examination of the accomplishments of public policy, which is known as the policy outcome, is equally significant. It helps us to understand how far the intended results have been achieved and whether the problems appearing from time to time have been overcome.

In the final analysis, the feedback of a public policy influences the future decisions of the government. Therefore, proper analysis of public policies enables the decision-makers to choose the right policy, allocate appropriate priorities and adopt efficient measures of implementation.

We have become more aware of the policy process as suitable object of study in its own right, primarily in the hope of improving the rationality of the flow of decisions. The study of public policy has attracted greater attention of the political scientists in the contemporary times as it analyses the causes and effects of governmental activities. The study of public policy involves an assessment of the impact of environmental forces on the content of public policy and an analysis of the effect of various institutional arrangements and political processes on public policy. It also includes an inquiry into the consequences of various public policies for the political system, and an evaluation of the impact of both expected and unexpected consequences. Politically, there are the difficulties faced by the democratic, federal structure in articulating clear and unambiguous goals. This vagueness of configuration of articulation is part of the interaction between the various political authorities ranging from the village to the central level, and the difficulties associated with future expenditure and resource use patterns are being inextricably linked to past decisions. There are also the ramifications flowing from the working of a mixed economy whereby the private sector policies are responsive to government actions. The need for coordinating various policy measures such as public and private adds another dimension to policy making.

Policy making in India has to take place in the context of a complex emerging and variegated society. Ant society has its own fundamentals, its own compulsions, and its own inner dynamics. The ambitious goals set for society have put it in a state of flux and change. The goals of reconstruction, including abolition of poverty, have led to increasing expectations and generated the need for rapid and orderly change. But any national advance has to be viewed within a framework of parameters flowing from (i) India being a democratic country, still an under developed third world nation, and (ii) India being a country of vast size and population giving it a continental dimension with its various regions, linguistic groups, cultural units, minorities, etc. Rising expectations and the goals set for itself by the state, when viewed in the context of the lack of resources, underline the need for attaining optimality in both the formulation and implementation of policy.

After the Second World War, the concept of the state in relation to its economic activities had undergone significant changes. The Union, the States and the Local Governments have increasingly participated in the economic and social functions. The state now intervenes to control and guide many activities.

The major goal of the state is social objective equalization with regard to basic services like education, public health and medical services. Since the commencement of the planning era in India in 1951, growth with social justice has been set forth as the cardinal principle of Indian planned economic development. Indian economy is a rural economy. The potential for progress and valuable resources lies in villages and not in a few metropolitan cities or municipal areas. In a predominantly agrarian economy like ours, the solution to massive problems of poverty and unemployment lies in the development of rural areas.

Ever since the country's independence, rural development has been one of the important thrusts of governmental policy. The constant effort of the government has been to develop the rural areas where the vast majority of the people live. But the kind of development and the amount of development, which have actually been realized, have been much below the planned aim of development. There has been no dearth of funds made available according to the allotment in different plans. The governmental policies have also been suitably modified from time to time. But the actual pace of development has been slow and much below expectation.

Development of rural areas has drawn attention of several Indian leaders as well as the intelligentsia in the early twenties. A few experiments were also attempted with little success, in rebuilding all rural parts of India. Despite a few experiments, the rural areas continued to be neglected. The steady increase of population, coupled with the alien rule during pre-independent times, were responsible for the neglect of rural India. Whatever progress was achieved in the past was confined to the urban parts. The benefits of progress did not reach the rural areas, particularly the rural poor. After independence, attention was focused on the theme of rural development and considerable efforts were made in that direction, both by the Union and State Governments.

Several studies had convincingly shown that the powerful section of the rural population and the better endowed segments had appropriated a disproportionately large share of the benefits of development efforts. In the process, rural poverty increased instead of decreasing and the weaker sections of the society, particularly among the rural areas, continued to lead a pathetic life.

The fundamental objective of rural development is to provide improved facilities like electrification, irrigation, communication, education, health care productivity, increased employment and higher income for the target groups, and technological changes in agriculture and allied sectors. This implies reducing poverty and human misery by increasing the productivity of the poorer sections and providing them greater access to goods and services. Further, rural development strategy needs to be explicitly identified with improving the overall quality of life of the poor masses. Rural development strategy is mainly motivated at achieving three fundamental goals:

(i) generation of self-employment opportunities in rural areas through programmes which are mainly intended to provide income-generating assets to people below the poverty line;

(ii) providing employment through programmes like the National Rural Employment Programme, Rural Landless Employment Guarantee Programme, Jawahar Rozgar Yojana, etc. and improving the skills of the rural people through training and providing basic needs like drinking water, sanitation and housing, etc.; and

(iii) the government has recognised that people's involvement should be ensured at every stage of the development programmes for a united effort in rural areas.

Since independence, the main thrust of plans and programmes in India has been the removal of poverty. It has been pointed out by a number of studies that poverty in India is concentrated among certain specific groups such as small farmers, agricultural labourers, Scheduled Castes, Backward Castes and Scheduled Tribes in the rural areas. Rural development denotes the development improvement in the economic and social condition of these downtrodden groups. Rural development is a dynamic concept which assumes significance in the context of socio-political and economic dualism in the developing countries and the efforts being made by the government to life the rural masses from poverty and deprivation.

Rural development also gains relevance due to the multitude of government's socio-economic programmes for the rural poor. The paramount aim of rural development is to improve the standard of living of the rural poor and raise then above the poverty line. Politicians and administrators in the developing countries have also evinced keen interest in learning and understanding the dimensions of rural problems and potentiality for alleviating rural poverty.

Rural development may be conceived as the development of infrastructural facilities for the people residing in the area. Allevation of rural poverty has been a major objective of the Seventh Five-Year Plan in India which aimed at bringing down the percentage of people below the poverty line. The approaches to the Eighth Plan gave much importance to the programmes aimed at giving self-employment and wage employment to the poorer sections of the community. During the First-Year Plan, two wage employment programmes, viz. NREP and RLEGP were in operation. From April 1989, both these programmes were merged into a single rural employment programme, known as Jawahar Rozgar Yojana. The primary objective of JRY is to generate additional gainful employment for the unemployed and underemployed persons, both men and women, in the rural areas. The secondary objectives of the JRY are to create sustained employment by strengthening rural economic infrastructure, to create community and social assets and also to create assets in favour of the rural poor, particularly the Scheduled Castes and Scheduled Tribes for their direct and continuing benefits which will improve the overall quality of life in the rural areas. The prevalence of unemployment and underemployment in the rural areas is a contributory factor for high incidence of poverty at the rural level. The JRY Programme has been given the main thrust to achieve the objective of poverty alleviation which in turn has led to its programme being directed towards the creation of various works to meet this objective.

The Zilla Praja Parishads and Village Panchayats are the two main functionaries for the implementation of JRY in Ranga Reddy district. Three Executive Engineers are functioning for three revenue divisions and 37 Mandals. The entire district is divided into 37 Revenue Mandals with 1055 villages and 583 Gram Panchayats. Among 1055 villages 982 are habitated villages and there are 73 unhabitated villages. The three Revenue Divisions are Hyderabad East, Chevella and Vikarabad. It may be observed that the performance of JRY in Ranga Reddy district is quite satisfactory. The performance of JRY in Ranga Reddy district relating to generation of physical man-days during 1995-96, 1996-97 and 1997-98 is phenomenol and it is significant to note that the achievement in employment generation is spectacular for it had exceeded the target fixed in this regard. It is significant to note that the district authorities are attaining above 100 per cent achievement.

It may be noted that the active participation of the people would help not only the target groups to avail themselves of the benefits that percolate from above, but also to articulate their demands and get what they need. The success of the public policy depends upon people's participation because increasing participation would rest on increasing awareness. In anti-poverty schemes like JRY, the participation of target groups is important for policy. In this regard, it may be observed that the target groups in Ranga Reddy district felt that government alone should take up these schemes because the government alone is competent enough to implement such schemes. It is significant to note that the rural poor in Ranga Reddy district are well aware of Jawahar Rozgar Yojana which is intended for rural upliftment and they are of the view that the JRY Programmes are within their easy reach.

The rural people in Ranga Reddy district maintain links with the elite groups of their villages. This reveals the quantum of their participation in the developmental schemes under Jawahar Rozgar Yojana. The participative dimension is dependent upon the cooperation that exists among the people. The analysis of data shows that the beneficiaries in Ranga Reddy district are of the view that the poor people should decide about the developmental schemes under Jawahar Rozgar Yojana.

Poverty is the result of landlessness and in addition to this the failure of monsoon, population exploitation, and bad habits among the downtrodden people, etc. are some of the other important causes for existence of poverty in villages and hence the analysis of data shows that 48.7 per cent (Table 4.15) respondents asked for increased assistance in the form of governmental programmes. The rural poor in Ranga Reddy district also pleaded for an increase in agricultural wages and that the rural unemployed and underemployed should be provided additional employment regularly for their economic upliftment. In this context, the analysis of data shows that 94.7 per cent (Table 4.17) of respondents strongly supported the Jawahar Rozgar Yojana because it is intended for the upliftment of the rural poor. The acceptance by a majority of respondents in regard to the benefits they received by JRY shows that the objectives of JRY are met in Ranga Reddy district and reflects the satisfactory implementation of JRY.

Generally, it is observed that the rural people depend on their village elite with the confidence that they pursue the developmental schemes and get them sanctioned from the government. The elite perception of Jawahar Rozgar Yojana in Ranga Reddy district reveals that the effective implementation of the Jawahar Rozgar Yojana schemes depends upon the training received by the officers handling JRY works at various levels and the government machinery must see that the rural elite at the district level should receive proper training in different aspects pertaining to Jawahar Rozgar Yojana. Every Gram Panchayat Office in Ranga Reddy district should invariably obtain a copy of the JRY manual for general information for the public. It may be observed that lack of required personnel may at times generate problems in the implementation of JRY. A majority of the elite in Ranga Reddy district have stated that there is an immense need for the recruitment of necessary staff for the effective implementation of JRY schemes and for the proper maintenance of record. Based on the experience in the implementation of JRY, the researcher has made an effort to suggest the following suggestions for the effective and qualitative implementation of Jawahar Rozgar Yojana in Ranga Reddy district.

(i) Gram Sabha meetings are to be held at least twice in a ear to discuss the action plan.

(ii) Delay in extending financial assistance to the beneficiaries should not be committed.

(iii) The funds provided under JRY may be enhanced keeping in view the hike in the cost of materials utilized under the developmental schemes.

(iv) Proper technical guidance may be provided to the beneficiaries and to the implementing officials to produce durable nature of works and to meet appropriate technical standards and specifications.

(v) The distribution of food grains under Jawahar Rozgar Yojana may be made optional depending upon the prices in the open market.

(vi) Village Panchayat should appoint a vigilance committee for each village under its jurisdiction to oversee, supervise and monitor the implementation of the works under the programme.

(vii) Sufficient care should be taken to ensure that the emergence of contractors in such devious ways is scrupulously avoided.

(viii) Both physical and financial audit of the works implemented by the Village Panchayats are to be made compulsory.

(ix) The details of works undertaken under JRY should be displayed on wall-posters or notice board at the Village Panchayat and Mandal office.

(x) Funds under JRY may be released, not based on the strength of population but on the poverty in the village.

It may be noted that the successful and effective implementation of the Jawahar Rozgar Yojana schemes depends upon the peaceful co-existence of the people and also on the clear-cut policy goals.

Bibliography

Abdul, Thana and Mumtaz Taha: *Manual on Integrated Rural Development*, A.A. Faizy, Sahada Manzil, Vliya Covil, Quilon, 1979.

Abida, Samiuddin: "The Emerging Pattern of Rural Leadership", *Kurukshetra*, Feb., 1977.

Abraham, A.: "Maharashtra's Employment Guarantee Scheme", *Economic and Political Weekly*, Aug. 9, 1980.

Acharya, K.R.: *Political Behaviour in Telangana: An Empirical Study of Preferences and Motivations during Parliamanetary Elections of 1971*, Unpublished Ph.D. Dissertation, J.N.U., New Delhi, 1979.

Adelman and Morries, C.T.: *Economic Growth and Social Equity in Developing Countries*, Standard University Press, 1973.

Adiseshaiah, Malcolm, S.: "Some Notes on Employment and Unemployment", *MIDS Bulletin*, Vol. V, No. 7, July, 1991.

Agarwala, R.N.: *National Movement and Constitutional Development of India*, Metropolitan Book Co., 1956.

Ali, Sofi: "Public Policy Making in India: Lessons from Rural Development Programmes", *Indian Journal of Public Administration*, Vol. 38, No. 2, Apr.-Jun., 1992.

Annual Reports of JRY 1989-1996, District Development Officer, Zilla Praja Parishad, Ranga Reddy District.

Apte, D.P.: "Crash Scheme for Rural Employment; Evaluation of the Programme in a District in Maharashtra", *Economic and Political Weekly*, March 24, 1973.

Bachenheimen, R.: "Elements of Leadership in an Andhra Villa" in *Leadership and Political Institutions in India*, Park, R.L. and Tinker, Princeton, 1959.

Bagchi, A.K.: "Planning for Employment", *Economic and Political Weekly*, Vol. XXV, No. 9, April, 1990.

Bajaj, J.L. and Shastri, C.T.: *Rural Poverty: Issue and Option*, Public Print House, 1985.

Bala Ramulu, C.H.: *Administration of Anti-Poverty Programmes (A Study of SFDA)*, Kakatiya School of Public Admn., Warangal, 1984.

Bala Subramanian, N.S.: "Seventh Plan and Rural Development", *Kurukshetra*, Vol. XXXIV, No. 9, May, 1986.

Bandopadhyaya, D.: *Study on Poverty Alleviation in Rural India Through Special Employment Creation Programmes*, AEP, New Delhi, 1986.

Banerjee, A.M. and Faquir Mohammad: "Policy Analysis and Development" in S.K. Sharma, *Dynamics of Development*, Concept Publishing Co., New Delhi, 1977.

Basu, K.: "Food for Work Programme: Beyond Roads that Get Washed Away", *Economic and Political Weekly*, Jan. 3, 1981.

Battacharya, B.B.: "Its Participatory Development Approach is Welcome", *Kurukshetra*, Vol. XL, No. 9, March, 1992.

Behari, Bipen: *Rural Poverty and Unemployment*, Vikas Publishing House, 1990.

Benninger, Anneta: "Village Eco-Development: Some Methodological Issues", *Social Change*, Vol. 22, No. 1, March, 1992.

Bhushan, Brij: "Role of Food Processing in Eradicating Rural Poverty and Unemployment", *Krukshetra*, Vol. XLII, No. 2, Nov., 1993.

Bipin Lehari: "Adopt Holistic Approach to Fight Poverty", *Kurkshetra*, Vol. XI, No. 1, Oct., 1991.

Carter, A.T.: *Elite Politics in Rural India*, Vikas Publishing House, 1975.

Census of India 1991, Govt. of India, New Delhi, 1992.

Chakravarthy, T.K.: *Development of Small and Marginal Farmers and Agricultural Labourers; An Overview of Policies and Programmes*, National Institute of Rural Development, Hyderabad, 1980.

Chamola, S.D.: "Revitalise PR Institutions to Plug Loopholes", *Kurkshetra*, Vol. XI, No. 1, Oct., 1991.

Chowdhary, Paul: "Reshape Development Strategy for Social Justice", *Kurukshetra*, Vol. XXIV, Oct., 1990.

Chowdhary, Ramesh Chandra: "Migration of Rural Labour: A Case Study of Samastpur District in Bihar", *Indian Journal of Labour Economics*, Vol. 34, No. 4, Oct.-Dec., 1991.

Concurrent Evaluation of JRY, Preliminary Report, Administrative Intelligence Division, Ministry of Rural Development, Krishi Bhavan, New Delhi, 1992.

Dandekar, K. and Sathe, M.: "Employment Guarantee Scheme and Food for Work Programme", *Economic and Political Weekly*, Vol. XV, No. 15, April 12, 1981.

Dandekar, V.M. and Neela Kantha Rath: *Poverty in India*, Indian School of Political Economy, Bombay, 1971.

Dantawala, M.L. et al.: "Search for an Employment oriented Wage Strategy (A Discussion)", *Economic and Political Weekly*, May 26, 1990.

Datar, Chhaya: "People Participation: An Important Component of JRY", *Kurukshetra*, Vol. XXXVIII, No. 4, Jan., 1990.

Derhgawen, R.K.: "Seven Steps for Success of RD Programmes", *Kurukshetra*, Vol. XL, No. 1, Oct., 1991.

Desai Ashok, V.: "Rural Development and Human Rights in Independent India", *Economic and Political Weekly*, Vol. XXII, No. 31, 1987.

Desai Ashok, V.: "Search for an Employment-oriented Growth Strategy (A Discussion)", *Economic and Political Weekly*, Vol. XXV, No. 21, May 26, 1990.

Desai, D.K.: *Management in Rural Development*, Oxford IBH Publishing Co., New Delhi, 1983.

Desai, Vasent: *Rural Development: Programmes and Strategies*, Vol. II, Himalaya Publishing House, Bombay, 1988.

Deshpande, K.S.: "A Brief Report on Functioning of JRY with Special Reference to Marathwada Region of Maharashtra", Paper Presented to National Work on JRY, NIRD, July, 1993.

Deshpande, L.K.: "Seventh Plan and Some Aspects of Employment", *Indian Economic Journal*, Vol. XXXIII, No. 4, Apr.-Jun., 1986.

Dhillon, H.S.: *Leadership and Groups in a South Indian Emerging Patterns of Rural Leadership in Southern Asia*, Planning Commission Programme Evolution Organisation, New Delhi, 1955.

Dhubesh, P.R.: *Rural Development Administration in India*, Popular Prakashan, Bombay, 1978.

Dutt, R.C.: "It's Corruption that Intercepts Rural Progress", *Kurukshetra*, Vol. XL, No. 1, Oct., 1991.

Dutt, Rudra and Sundaram, K.P.M.: *Indian Economy*, Chand & Co., New Delhi, 1989.

Dye Thomas, R. and Harman Zeiglar: *The Irony of Democracy*, Princeton Hall Inc., Englewood Cliff, New Jersey, Wordsworth Belment, California, 1970.

Dye Thomas, R.: *Policy Analysis*, Princeton Hall Inc., Englewood Cliff, New Jersey, University of Alabama Press, Alabama, 1976.

Dye Thomas, R.: *Understanding of Public Policy*, Princeton Hall Inc., Englewood Cliff, New Jersey, Chand & Co., New Delhi, 1972.

Earl, Latham: "The Group Basis of Politics" in Eulau, Heinz, et al. (Eds.), *Political Behaviour*, Free Press, New York, 1956.

Easton, David: *A System Analysis of Political Life*, Willey, New York, 1965.

Easton, David: *The Political System*, Knopf, New York, 1953.

Engine, T.: "Jawahar Rozgar Yojana", *Southern Economist*, Vol. XXVIII, No. 9, Sept., 1989.

G.O. 17040/NREP.111/89 dated Jun. 20, 1989, R.D. Dept. New Delhi.

G.O. No. 87080/NREP/111/89-1 dt. Dec. 28, 1989, Rural Development Dept., Govt. of India, Hyderabad.

George, P.: "Employment Generation: Early Experiments", Paper Presented to National Workshop on JRY, NIRD, July, 1990.

Ghate, P.T.: *Direct Attacks on Rural Poverty, Policy, Programmes and Implementation*, Concept Publishers, New Delhi, 1984.

Ghosh, B.N.: "Public Policy: A Conceptual Note", *Indian Journal of Public Administration*, Vol. 38, No. 1, Jan.-Mar., 1992.

Ghosh, D.K.: "Monitoring and Rural Development Programmes—Some Issues", *Kurukshetra*, Vol. XXXIX, No. 6, March, 1991.

Government Andhra Pradesh: *Towns and Municipalities: A Handbooks of Statistics—Ranga Reddy District 1996—97*, 1981.

Government of Andhra Pradesh: *Guidelines for JRY*, Secretary, Department of Panchayat Raj and Rural Development, Hyderabad, 1990.

Government of Andhra Pradesh: *Handbook of Statistics of Ranga Reddy District*, Office of the Chief Planning Officer, Ranga Reddey District, Hyderabad, 1996.

Government of Andhra Pradesh: *Jawahar Rozgar Yojana Open Wells Scheme Instructions*, AP Scheduled Castes Co-operative Finance Corporation, Hyderabad, 1992.

Government of India: *Concurrent Evaluation of NREP: The Main Findings of the Survey*, Ministry of Agriculture, New Delhi, 1988.

Government of India: *Five Year Plans (I-V), 1952, 1957, 1961, 1969 and 1974*, Planning Commission, New Delhi.

Government of India: *India; A Reference Annual 1976*, New Delhi, 1976.

Government of India: *JRY Manual*, As Modified and Effective from 1.4.1991, Ministry of Agriculture, Dept. of Rural Development, New Delhi, June, 1991.

Government of India: *JRY Manual*, Draft Guidelines, Ministry of Agriculture, Dept. of Rural Development, New Delhi, April, 1989.

Government of India: *National Rural Employment Programme: A Guidelines*, Ministry of Rural Reconstruction, New Delhi, 1983.

Government of India: *Sixth Five Year Plan 1980-85*, Planning Commission, New Delhi, 1981.

Gracious Thomas: "How Far People Participate in Rural Development", *Economic and Political Weekly*, Vol. XXVIII, No. 26, July 26, 1993.

Gupta, Ranjeet: "Rural Works Programme: Where its has gone Astray", *Economic and Political Weekly*, Vol. VI, No. 20, May, 1971.

Gupta, Sanjay Das: "Workshop Report: JRY—A Critical Review", *Institute of Rural Management*, New Delhi, 1990.

Gurumurthy, V.: *Panchayati Raj and the Weaker Sections*, Ashish Publishing House, 1987.

Hancha Chopra and Gopal, K. Kedekody: "The Water-shed Development", *Kurukshetra*, Vol. XL, No. 4, Jan., 1992.

Hanumanth Rao, C.H.: "Integrating Poverty Alleviation Programme with Development Strategies: Indian Experience", *Economic and Political Weekly*, Vol. XXVII, No. 192, Jul.-Dec., 1990.

Haque, T.: "Strategy for Ful Employment in Rural India", IASSI, Vol. IX, No. 192, Jul.-Dec., 1990.

Hara Gopal, G. and Bala Ramulu: "Poverty Alleviation Programmes", *Economic and Political Weekly*, Vol. XIV, Nos. 35-36, Sept.-Dec., 1989.

Hara Gopal, G.: *Administrative Leadership and Rural Development in India*, Life and Light Publishers, New Delhi, 1980.

Harichandran, C.: Panchayat Raj and Rural Development, Concept Publishing Co., New Delhi, 1983.

Hirway, Indira.: *Abolition of Poverty in India: A Study of Target Group Approach*, Vikas Publishing House, New Delhi, 1986.

Hirway, Indira: "Panchayati Raj at Cross Roads", *Economic and Political Weekly*, July 22, 1989.

Hirway, Indira: "Seven Proged Strategy to Make Administration Responsive", *Kurukshetra*, Vol. XI, No. 1, Oct., 1991.

Hirway, Indira: *Wage Employment Programme in India: A Study of NREP in Gujarat*, Oxford and IBH Publishing Co., New Delhi, 1986.

James, E. Anderson: *Public Policy Making*, Praegar Publishers, New York, 1975.

Jayaraj: "Rural Development Strategy", *Yojana*, Vol. XXXVII, No. 3, Feb., 16-28, 1991.

Jha, S.K.: *Rural Development Administration in India*, Janaki Prakashan, New Delhi, 1988.

Johi, Navin Chandra: "JRY to Usher in Rural Rejuvenation", *Kurukshetra*, Vol. XXXVII, No. 4, Jan., 1990.

Kakwani, N. and K. Subba Rao: "Rural Poverty and its Alleviation in India", *Economic and Political Weekly*, Vol. XXV, No. 13, March 31, 1990.

Kar, G.C.: "Poverty: Some Conceptual Considerations", *Journal and Rural Development*, Vol. VIII, No. 3, May, 1989.

Key, V.O. Jr.: *Public Opinion: American Democracy*, Knopf, New York, 1967.

Khan, Akhter Hameed: *Ten Decades of Rural Development: Lessons from India*, Michigan State University, 1978.

Krishnan, T.N.: "Population, Poverty and Employment in India", *Economic and Political Weekly*, Vol. XXVII, No. 46.

Kukherji, A.B. and Ahmad, A. (eds.): *India: Culture, Society and Economy*, Inter India Publications, 1986.

Kukherji, S.: *Essays on Rural Development*, Utsargo Publications, Varanasi, 1982.

Kurien, C.T.: *Poverty Planning and Social Transformation*, Allied Publishers, New Delhi, 1990.

Lasswell, Harold D. and Abraham Kaplan: *Power and Society*, Yale University Press, New Heaven, 1970.

Lasswell, Harold D.: "Public Policy Orientatioan" in Learner, D. and Lasswell, H.D. (Ed.), *The Policy Science*, Standford, California, 1971.

Lee, Ronald F. et al.: *Population, Food and Rural Development*, Clarendon Press, Oxford, 1991.

Lindblom, Charles E.: "The Science of Muddling Through", *Public Administration Review*, Vol. XIX, No. 12, Sept., 1992.

Linga, Murthy, N.: "Working of National Rural Employment Programme in A.P.—A Study", *Kurukshetra*, Vol. XXXIV, No. 56, Feb., 1986.

Maddick, H.: *Panchayat Raj: A Study of Rural and Local Govt. in India*, Longmans, London, 1978.

Mahajan, V.S.: "JRY: Economic and Experience", Paper Presented to National Workshop on JRY, NIRD, July, 1993.

Mahajan, V.S.: *Planning and Socialistic Transformation of Indian Economy*, Deep & Deep Publishers, New Delhi, 1983.

Mahajan, V.S.: *Studies in Indian Agriculture and Rural Development*, Deep & Deep Publishers, New Delhi, 1986.

Mahajan, V.S.: *Studies in Indian Economy*, Deep & Deep Publishers, New Delhi, 1983.

Maheshwari, Hari Prakash and Arun Kumar Gard: "GRY: A Case Study", *Yojana*, Vol. XXXV, No. 5, March, 16-31, 1991.

Maheshwari, S.R.: *Rural Development in India*, Sage Publication, New Delhi, 1985.

Markanandan, N.: "A New Approach to Rural Development", *Kurukshetra*, Vol. XLI, No. 10, July, 1993.

Mathur, B.S.: *Planning and the Poor*, S. Chand & Co., New Delhi, 1978.

Mathur, M.V.: *Panchayat Raj in Rajasthan: A Case Study of Jaipur District*, Impex India, New Delhi, 1966.

Meghe, D.R. and Rajput, R.S.: *Panchayat Raj in India—Democracy at Grassroots*, Deep & Deep Publications, New Delhi, 1984.

Mehta Uday: "The Impact of the Panchayat Raj on Rural India" in *Rural Socialism in India*, 5th Edition, Popular Prakashan, 1978.

Memo No. 35090-NREP.111/89 July 10, 1989, Rural Development Dept., Govt. of India, New Delhi.

Memo No. 69693/E.VI/91, dt. Nov. 25, 1991, Panchayat Raj and Rural Development, Hyderabad.

Michael, Teitz: "Towards a Theory of Urban Public Facility Location", Paper of the Regional Science Association, No. 21, 1968.

Minhas, B.S.: *Planning and the Poor*, S. Chand & Co., New Delhi, 1978.

Mishra, S.: *Constitutional Development and National Movement in India*, Janaki Prakasan, Patna, 1978.

Mishra, S.N.: "Emerging Leadership in Rural India: A Case Study", *Quarterly Journal of the Local Self-Government Institution*, Vol. XVII, No. 2, Oct.-Dec., 1976.

Mosor and Kalton, C.A.: *Survey Methods to Social Investigation*, Heinemann Education Book Ltd., London, 1971.

Munger, Frank J.: "Opinion, Elections, Parties and Policies: A Prostrage Analysis", Paper Delivered at Annual Meetings of the American Political Association, New York, 1960.

Muralidhar Rao, A.: "Renewed Approach of Jawahar Rozgar Yojana," *Kurukshetra*, Vol. XL, No. 2, April, 1991.

Muthayya, B.C., Krishnama Naidu, K., and Anneruddin, M.: *Behavioural Dimensions of Rural Leaders*, National Institute of Rural Development, Hyderabad, 1979.

Myrdal, Gunnar: *An Approach to the Asian Drama: Methodological and Theoretical*, Vintage Books, London, 1970.

Narain, I. Panday, K.C. and Sharma, M.L.: *The Rural Elite in an Indian State: A Case Study of Rajasthan*, Manohar Book Service, New Delhi, 1976.

Narain, Iqbal: "Democratic Decentralisation and Rural Leadership in India—Rajasthan Experiment", *Asian Survey*, Vol. IV, No. 8, 1964.

Narain, Iqbal: *From Dyaschy to Self-Government*, Shivelal Agarwal & Co., Agra, 1950.

Narayana, D.L.: "The Rural Development Programme and Poverty Eradication", Paper Presented to a Seminar on NREP and RLEGP, Ministry of Rural Development, Govt. of India, Feb., 27-28, 1989.

Narula, Renu: "JRY with Reference to VP", *Rural India*, No. 53, Feb., 1990.

NSS 38th Round: "Results of the Third Quinnial Survey on Employment and Unemployment", *Sarvkshana*, Vol. XI, No. 4, April, 1968.

Ordway, Tead: *The Art of Leadership*, McGraw Hill Book, Co., New York, 1963.

Padhy, Kishore Chandra: *Rural Development in Modern India*, D.R. Publishing Corporation, New Delhi, 1979.

Panda, M.K.: "Productivity Aspects of Wages in FFWP", *Economic and Political Weekly*, May 16, 1981.

Pankert, Fles: "Income Distribution at Different Levels of Development: A Survey of Evidence", *International Labour Review*, Aug., 1973.

Parvathama: "Panchayat Raj and Weaker Sections", Presented at the Seminar held at NIRD, Hyderabad, 1975.

Paulin, V. Young and Calvin F. Schmid: *Scientific Social Surveys and Research*, Prentice Hall of India, New Delhi, 1975.

Planning Commission: *Employment, Past Trends and Prospects for 1990*, Government of India, New Delhi, 1990.

Ram Reddy, G. and Hara Gopal, G.: "The Pairavikar and the Rural Fixer", *Asian Survey*, Vol. XXV, No. 11, Nov., 1985.

Ram Reddy, G. and Hara Gopal, G.: *Public Policy and Rural Poor in India*, Concept Publishing Co., New Delhi, 1985.

Ram Reddy, G.: *The Patterns of Panchayat Raj in India*, Macmillan & Co., New Delhi, 1977.

Randhawa, M.S.: *Developing Village India*, Orient Longman, Bombay, 1951.

Ranney, Austin (ed.): *Political Science and Public Policy*, Markhan, Chicago, 1968.

Rao, M.S.A.: *Urbanisation and Social Change*, Orient Longman, Bombay, 1972.

Rao, Narasimha, P.V.: "Democratic Discipline—Must for Success of Constitution (73rd Amendment) Act, 1992", *Kurukshetra*, Vol. XLI, No. 12, Sept., 1993.

Rao, Narasimha, P.V.: What 8th Plan should Achieve", *Kurukshetra*, Vol. XL, No. 5, Feb., 1992.

Rao, Pandit, Y.A.: "Some Issues Relating to Rural Unemployment", *Khadi Gramodyog*, Vol. XXXVII, No. 1, Oct., 1990.

Rao, Ranga, S.P.: "Give Panchayats Operational Freedom under JRY", *Kurukshetra*, Vol. XXXVIII, No. 4, Jan., 1990.

Reddy, D.N.: "A Note on Employment Guarantee Scheme: The Maharashtra Experience and Lessons", *Indian Journal of Labour Economics*, Jan., 1982.

Robert, Evestone: *The Thread of Public Policy: A Study in Policy Leadership*, Boobs-Merri, Indianapolise, 1971.

Roberties, Babcock: *State and Local Government Politics*, Random House, New York, 1957.

Rose, Richard (Ed.): *Policy Making in Great Britain*, Macmillan Co., London, 19, 1991.

Royan, Bunker: "Why not Try the District Pool Strategy", *Kurukshetra*, Vol. XL, No. 1, Oct., 1991.

Sahni, Pradeep: *Public Policy: Conceptual Dimensions*, Kitab Mahal, Allahabad, 1987.

Sajal, Krishnan: Policy Making in India, Vikas Publishing House, Pvt. Ltd., New Delhi, 1983.

Sanwel, Mukul: "Panchayati Raj the Next Steps," *Economic and Political Weekly*, Vol. XXIV, No. 42, October 21, 1989.

Sastry, S.A.R.: *Level and Patterns of A.P.*, Sardar Patel Institute for Economic and Social Research, 1979.

Seshadri, M.: *Political Linkages and Rural Development*, National Publishing House, New Delhi, 1976.

Shaffir, Cheema G. (ed.): *Rural Development in Asia: Case Studies on Programme Implementation*, Sterling Publishers, New Delhi, 1985.

Shah, D.R.: *Alternatives in Rural Development*, Sterling Publishers, New Delhi, 1990.

Shah, S.M.: "Are Panchayats Ready for JRY", *Kurukshetra*, Vol. XXXVIII, No. 4, Jan., 1990.

Shah, S.M.: "Where have Failed in Rural Development", *Kurukshetra*, Vol. XL, No. 1, Oct., 1991.

Sharma, D.P. and Desai, V.V.: *Rural Economy of India*, Vikas Publishing House, New Delhi, 19, 1980.

Shekhar, Iyer: "JRY: A Job at Doorstep", *Economic and Political Weekly*, Vol. XXXVII, No. 10, July, 1989.

Shivaiah, M. et al.: *Panchayat Raj Elections in Andhra Pradesh*, NIRD, Hyderabad, 1981.

Shourie, Arun: "Growth, Poverty and Inequality", *Foreign Affairs*, Jan. 2, 1973.

Singh, et al.: NREP: Performance Prospect", *Journal of Rural Development*, Vol. VIII, No. 1, Jan., 1989.

Singh, Mahinder: *Rural Development Administration and Anti-Poverty Programme*, Deep & Deep Publications, New Delhi, 1988.

Singh, R.B.: *Geography of Rural Development*, Inter India Publications, New Delhi, 1986.

Singh, R.L. and Singh Rana, P.B.: *Rural Development in India in Environment*, N.G.S.I. Publications, Varanasi, 1977.

Singh, Tarlok: "Employment and Planning Assessment and Strategies in India", *Indian Economic Journal*, Apr.-Jun., 1976.

Sinha, R.K.: *Economic Development and Social Change in India*, Deep & Deep Publications, New Delhi, 1985.

Sirsikar, V.M.: *The Rural Elite in a Developing Society*, Orient Longmans, New Delhi, 1970.

Siva Subramanyam, K.: "Background Papers in JRY", Paper Presented in National Workshop on JRY, NIRD, July, 1993.

Sodhi, J.S.: "Jawahar Rozgar Yojana: Panacea for Rural Development", *Economic Times*, June 10, 1989.

Somasekhara, N.: *Rural Energy*, Sterling Publishers Pvt., Ltd., New Delhi, 1985.

Srinivan, S.: "Rural Development Programme in the Mid-80s", *Khadigramodyog*, Vol. XXXVI, No. 4, Jan. 10, 1990.

Srinivasan, T.N. and Burdhan, P.K. (Ed.): *Poverty and Income Distributing in India*, Statistical Publishing Society, Calcutta, 1987.

Srivastava, M. and Singh, A.K. (Eds.): *Rural Development in India*, Deep & Deep Publications, New Delhi, 1987.

Subramanya, K.N.: *Economic Development and Planning in India*, Deep & Deep Publications, New Delhi, 1985.

Sudhir, Krishna: "To the Grassroots", *Seminar*, Vol. 413, Annual, Jan., 1994.

Tadaro, Michael, P.: *Economies for a Developing World*, Longmans Group Ltd. London, 1977.

Thakur, Devendhra: *Rural Development and Planning in India*, Deep & Deep Publications, New Delhi, 1989.

Town Send, P. (Ed.): *The Concept of Poverty*, Heinemann Publishers, London, 1985.

Tripathi, Brajesh Pati: "Securing People's Participation in Rural Development through Panchayati Raj (A Cricital Appraisal)", *Kurukshetra*, Vol. XLI, No. 4, Jan., 1993.

Truman David, B.: *The Governmental Process*, Knopf, New York, 1951.

United Nations: *Development Administration: Current Approaches and Trends in Public Administration for National Development, Department of Economic and Social Affairs*, United Nations, New York, 1975.

Visaria, Pravin: "Poverty and Unemployment in India: An Analysis of Recent Evidence", *World Development*, Vol. IX, No. 3, March, 1981.

Vohra, I.A.: "Status Paper on JRY—Gujarat" Presented to National Workshop on JRY at NIRD, July, 1993.

Wedderbun, Dorothy. (Ed.): *Poverty, Inequality and Class Structure*, Cambridge University Press, London, 1974.

World Bank: *India: Poverty, Employment and Social Service*, Washington, 1989.

Index